Behind Lesbia's Door
Her Slave-Girls' Shocking Revelations

~~~

The 700-Year-Old Mystery of Catullus's Song-Poem 67 Solved *via* Cicero's *Pro Caelio*

~~~

Gaetano Catelli

Clodia is no ordinary woman and colliding with her Catullus has struck off poems which are not ordinary. (Thornton Wilder)

Do not look again, as before, for my love,
which you casually castrated
like a flower at a meadow's edge –
sliced by a passing plough.
(Gaius "the Puppy" Catullus)

The worst *poet* ever!
(Clodia "the Beautiful" Metelli)

Front cover: model: Marisa Rojo; door: *Roma*
Back cover: *il Colosseo*
Font: Bookman Oldstyle

ISBN-13: 978-0615654805

Dedication

To Miss Elizabeth Coates and Miss Ruth Yergin

gratias maximas tibi ago

Preface

*[I]f my meaning is different from, or even contradictory to, yours,
have we done anything but demonstrate the essential richness of
the poem in question? Certainly a plurality of meanings is better
than no meaning at all.* (Frank Copley)

The brain is a physical organ. As with the heart, lungs, and muscular system, a program of regular vigorous mental exercise will optimize the brain's performance. It is virtually never too soon, nor too late, to begin such a program. The most efficient way, though not the only one, of conducting a program of systematic brain exercise is through formal education. The study of the ancient classics, because the original texts are in a language unfamiliar to modern readers, constitutes a particularly rigorous regimen of brain exercise.

The question of whether such study will lead to a job, though it may, nevertheless misses the larger point, just as would asking the same question about working-out at the gym. *The primary purpose of engaging in the study of the humanities, particularly the ancient classics, is personal transformation –* from a merely clever hominid into a cultivated human being. In response to charges that this constitutes an elitist agenda, it may be replied that it is not an elitism based upon ancestry, social standing, or inherited wealth, but rather upon an individual's own blood, sweat, and tears.

In today's world, and assuredly tomorrow's, jobs will come and go. But, the transformation wrought by an education in the humanities will remain.

My only formal instruction in Latin was provided during six years of secondary schooling, via the heroically patient exertions of Miss Elizabeth Coates and Miss Ruth Yergin. Some half of a century afterward, I was a photographer of glamour models in the Soho district of New York City. A photograph I captured of an especially gifted model and painter, Amber Miller Carr, reminded me of a two-line *Carmen* <song-poem> by Catullus (85, as I soon rediscovered).

iv

I took from my bookshelf the dusty Latin dictionary I had purchased decades earlier (because you never know), and proceeded to (liberally) translate it thus:

odi et amo faciam requiris
nescio sed fieri sentio et excrucior

I *loathe* – and yet I *worship*. "How so?" – you ask.
I don't know; but I feel crucified and cremated.

Soon, a photograph I took of psychotherapist Victoria Zdrok inspired me to translate *Carmen* 5, which begins *vivamus mea lesbia atque amemus* ... <Let's live and let's love, my Lesbia ... >. When finished, I was struck by the thought: I can *still do* this! The transformation has been permanent.

I translated several more of Catullus's song-poems on an *ad hoc* basis, eventually deciding to translate them all. Along the way, I read a comment by classicist Christian James Fordyce (pp. xvi-xvii):

If we do not know who Lesbia was, that does not greatly matter; what matters far more is [Catullus's] passion of such loyal intensity that ... she has survived the centuries with him.

But, by looking through the other end of the telescope (a reflex I acquired from studying mathematics), it occurred to me that the reverse is more the case: *Catullus* has achieved literary immortality by writing about *Clodia Metelli* – and thus, it does greatly matter, as shall be shown, that she is the "Lesbia" of Catullus's song-poems of loathing and worship. (In accord, "Lesbia in Old Age", p. 7 below)

As a consequence of this insight, I have since embarked upon writing a biography of Clodia Metelli, the working title of which is: Our *Lesbia: First Lady of the Roman Empire and Great Mother to the New Poets*. When completed, this volume will contain, with accompanying commentary, a new translation of Cicero's oration, *Pro Caelio*, in which he thunderously denounces Clodia's morals (as *he* perceives them); those portion's of Cicero's private correspondence in which Clodia is referenced (a much more nuanced picture); and the entirety of the surviving Catullan corpus.

The work herein, which explicates my reading of Catullus's *Carmen* 67 ("The Door"), is an excerpt from this work in progress. To avoid giving rise to distraction, it does not contain the two photographs that are the seeds from which this enterprise has grown, but these photographs will adorn the front and back covers, respectively, of the completed biography of Clodia.

(Note to teachers, past and current: Had it been suggested to Miss Coates and Miss Yergin that I would someday write a monograph on *Carmen* 67, and had they been of a more demonstrative nature, each would likely have fallen to the floor in fits of laughter. Sometimes seeds bear fruit though planted in apparently barren soil.)

The present work is organized into two parts: The first is intended to be accessible to any reader of literature (with or without formal study of Latin) who has had some exposure to a college-level education.

The second part addresses in some detail various scholarly controversies that have arisen over what constitutes the most coherent reading of song-poem 67, including controversies over the correct wording of the Latin text itself. I have endeavored to make this section likewise accessible to general readers. Hence, there is more repetition than would otherwise be the case; words and phrases are translated that typically are left untranslated; terms are spelled out that usually are abbreviated; and the Index includes a number of glossary-like parenthetic notes, as well as cross-references to authors who appear in the Works Cited section. Inevita-bly, though, the second part will be of greater interest to specialists.

Timothy Peter Wiseman[1] begins his illuminating *Catullus and His World: A Reappraisal*:

> Of all the Latin poets, Catullus is the one who seems to speak most directly to us .... I think we have been too easily satisfied with an illusory Catullus ...

I can speak with assurance only of my personal experience: As a wee lad barely on this side of puberty (wholly innocent of any "nineteenth-century reconstruction", illusory or not), when Miss Coates first introduced our 9th grade class to Catullus,

I was thunderstruck.

Though it is highly speculative to suggest, recent neurological research is not inconsistent with the view that in reading literature, or in hearing it (or other aural arts) spoken, it may be that the reader/listener's neurons are firing synchronously with those of the original author or a subsequent performer.

If so, it may be that there is a plausible physical basis for believing that in reading or reciting Cicero's prose or Catullus's poesy, we react physiologically, and hence emotionally, as we would if we were in the Roman Senate House hearing Cicero denounce Clodia's brother Clodius, or with Catullus and the orator Calvus whilst they are composing song-poems together.

To put the matter straightforwardly: The spirit of Clodia, Clodius, Catullus, Caelius, and Cicero, *inter alia*, in some literal sense perhaps dwells in each of us who reads/recites the words they have written, or even that have been written about them.[2] For myself, at any rate, they are as much a part of my present as any living figure outside of my immediate purview.

Hence, this work is written in the historical present. Other stylistic tics include Promiscuity in Capitalization, parsimony in punctuation, a love of alliteration, a sense for assonance, an inclination for anaphora, no dislike of litotes, and permissiveness *vis-à-vis* dangling participles (good enough for Cicero → good enough for me).

That said, citations for the most part are contained within the body of the text; the endnotes mainly contain expanded discussion of points made in the text and/or internet links to primary sources. Sprinkled among the text and endnotes are web-links to so-called 'pop classics' of the past century that further illustrate *why* "... Catullus is the one who seems to speak most directly to us". All links accessed July 31, 2012.

Since both Catullus's song-poems and Cicero's *Pro Caelio* were originally read aloud, italicization is liberally employed to suggest *vocal* emphasis.

To my knowledge, texts in the Late Republic appear in all-lowercase or ALL-UPPERCASE, without punctuation. Latin text herein is presented accordingly, because I find that the selective capitalization and punctuation imposed upon the Latin text by scholars sometimes narrow possible read-ings more than Catullus, in particular, may have intended.

Non-English words or phrases are followed by translation with-in <angle brackets>. Translation of such words that appear within quotation of another author are presented within [<angle brackets that are within square brackets>].

All translations are my own, save those from ancient Greek by Bernadotte Perrin (Plutarch's *Parallel Lives*), by Earnest Cary (Cassius Dio's *Roman History*), and a few other cases that are noted as such.

As far as I am aware, my translations of passages from arti-cles by Ugo Carratello and Giuseppe Billanovich are the first to appear in English; and, my translation of the poem frag-ment by the 9th century theologian Ildemaro (Hildemar), which is quoted in Billanovich's article, is the first to appear in any modern language.

Special thanks for assistance and inspiration by Angela Bruno; Audrey Hepbourne; Ayumi Sakamoto; Barbara Lagfarr; Brian Mazur, PhD; Brooke Allen; Bruce Wood, LCSW; BTC Grocery; Charles Gross, PhD; Christian Sellar, PhD; Damien Mire; Dániel Kiss, PhD; David Campanella; Elizabeth Spivey, MFA; Giulia Trojer; High Point Coffee; JD Williams Library, Uni-versity of Mississippi; John Conlon, PhD; Lauren Dayan; Lindsey Etheridge, JD; Morgan Pennington; New York Public Library; Oxford Public Library; Rei Ichikawa; Ronald Primas, MD; Sarah Jacobs; Sally Lineback; Scott Clark; Scott Ken-yon; Square Books; Vera Pa; and Victoria Zdrok, PhD, JD.

For further study (in chronological order): the aforementioned TP Wiseman's *Catullus and His World: A Reappraisal* provides a dense and wide-ranging discussion of the context of the works of Catullus and of Cicero's *Pro Caelio*. Peter Green's *Catullus: A Bilingual Edition* offers a Latin text closely based upon Mynor's (I, in turn, have relied upon Green's text) and his own translation that well captures the Catullan spirit, with concise but very informative annotations and glossary. Julia Dyson Hejduk's *Clodia: A Sourcebook* presents her lucid and accurate translations of Cicero's *Pro Caelio* and those of his private letters in which Clodia is referenced. Marilyn Skinner's *Clodia Metelli: The Tribune's Sister* perceptively discusses virtually every reference to Clodia contained in the ancient sources. All of these volumes are highly readable.

A final note: William Butler Yeats, one of the great poets of the Irish Literary Revival, was much influenced by Catullus's work. Out of his interest in Catullus, he wrote a poem that is well-known among classicists, "The Scholars" (original version):

> Bald heads forgetful of their sins,
> Old, learned, respectable bald heads
> Edit and annotate the lines
> That young men, tossing on their beds,
> Rhymed out in love's despair
> To flatter beauty's ignorant ear.
> All shuffle there; all cough in ink;
> All wear the carpet with their shoes;
> All think what other people think;
> All know the man their neighbour knows.
> Lord, what would they say
> Did their Catullus walk that way?

It barely requires comment that without many brilliant scholars coughing ink while they paced the carpet over the course of the centuries, we would not have an intelligible Catullan text at all. My aim is not to disparage their invaluable contributions to high culture, but rather to invite readers to join with me in peering through the other end of the telescope.

With my limited background in scholarship generally, and Latin in particular, I cannot possibly approach the level of erudition and insight of professional classicists. But, there is one circumstance that has informed my studies of Clodia and Catullus that I ask readers to believe, if nothing else:

I *walked* the *walk*.

Gaetano Catelli
Oxford, Mississippi; March 15, 2012.

Website: www.gallerialesbia.com
Facebook: www.facebook.com/636441322
Twitter: @LesbiasSparrow

Notes on Six Translations of 67:19-22

There is a double-bind for translators of any poet's work, no less so for Catullus: A literal translation lacks the smooth polish a poet such as Catullus achieves in the original Latin. Yet, a polished translation that flows smoothly for modern ears and eyes results in substituting a contemporary tuxedo for Catullus's tunic. Alas, all too often a translation that attempts to balance the two falls short in both respects.

Thus, a translation completely true to Catullus's poetry has been deemed "impossible" by poet and critic Ezra Pound, who adds for good measure: "I have failed forty times myself so I do know the matter."

The dilemma is not as pronounced for the translator of Cicero's prose. Ever the advocate, Cicero's intent is to persuade (often, even in private correspondence); therefore, though not completely absent, allusion and wordplay obscure to modern readers is not omnipresent in Cicero's writings. While no one would confuse Cicero's prose style with, say, Ernest Hemingway's, the task of translating Cicero's prose is less daunting than translating Catullus's.

It is unsurprising, then, that a notable passage from one of Cicero's letters to his close friend Atticus is translated very similarly by two different scholars, though their efforts are separated by more than a century.

The Latin text reads:

> *reginae fuga mihi non molesta est clodia quid egerit scribas ad me*

British scholar Evelyn Shirley Shuckburgh (died 1906) translates it thus <u>xrl.us/bm46ep</u>:

> I am not sorry for the Queen's [*ie,* Cleopatra's] flight.
> I should like you to tell me what Clodia has done.

American scholar Hejduk (2008, p. 61) renders it:

> I'm not worried about the queen's flight. I'd like you to write me what Clodia has done.

Hejduk's translation of this passage is commendably more faithful to the Latin text:

[M]olesta is akin to 'mental molestation', hence "worry" *about*, rather than "sorrow" *for*. Instead of Shuckburgh's implication that Cicero is glad Cleopatra is gone from Rome (though no doubt true), Hejduk's literal rendering could imply that Cicero is denying that Cleopatra's flight from Rome, in the wake of Julius Caesar's assassination, might be an ominous portent for his own safety. (If so, Cicero's denial may be 'whistling past the graveyard' – he himself is assassinated 20 months later.)

[S]cribas is ancestor to "scribe"; thus, "write" is a more accurate rendering than "tell".

Perhaps because contractions are shunned in formal writing a century ago, Shuckbaugh chooses "I am" and "I should", instead of Hejduk's "I'm" and "I'd". But, Hejduk's choice is arguably again more accurate, though in this case only relatively so. It is true that personal pronouns are not explicit in this passage; instead they are implicit in the ending of the verbs. Hejduk's contractions do capture this compression. However Cicero's text does not contain, explicitly or implicitly, the first-person singular "I am" or "I'm". Instead, *fuga* <flight> is the subject of *non molesta est* <has not been worrying me>, not an object of either "for" or "about". Nonetheless, the meaning seems equivalent in either rendering.

However, *egerit* <done> does have alternate shades of meaning (though perhaps indeterminate in the context in which it occurs here). Syntactically, *egerit* may be either third-person singular perfect active subjunctive, or third-person singular future-perfect active indicative. Shuckburgh and Hejduk adopt the former, which implies two things: that Cicero uses here the 'subjunctive by attraction' because of *egerit's* proximity to the optative *scribas;* and, of more import, in this reading Cicero assumes that Clodia has *already* done *something,* and wants Atticus to relate to him what that something is.

I have chosen instead to read *clodia quid egerit* as future-perfect, which is less restrictive in meaning, ie, "what Clodia *shall* have done". This rendering implies that Cicero is unsure that Clodia has yet done *anything,* though he *expects* she will do something. This, I think, is in keeping with the fluid and uncertain nature of that time in Rome: Mobs infuriated by the assassination of the populist Caesar a mere month earlier have been roaming the City seeking to wreak vengeance upon their rulers (resulting in the killing of Cinna the Poet, among others). Cleopatra has fled; Clodia herself may be in jeopardy. (Cp. Skinner's suggestion, n. 46 below.)

Hence, my translation reads:

> The Queen's flight has not been worrying me. About Clodia: Whatever she shall have done, I would that you write to me.

Though written a century apart, the very similar translations of Shuckburgh and Hejduk read and sound natural to Anglophone ears. My translation instead sounds stuffy and formal. However, my sense is that Cicero is a stuffy and formal sort of Roman. I cannot hear the 'voice' of Cicero in their translations. Though it is only in my imagination, I can hear Cicero's voice in my own.

In marked contrast to Shuckbaugh's and Hejduk's respective translations of Cicero, I have yet to read two translations of Catullus both of which sound as if originally written by the same underlying poet. By way of example, there follows a four-line excerpt from song-poem 67, with a literal prose translation by Skinner, and verse translations by four others – these presented in chronological order of publication. The context is the gossip of the front door of a house, personified as a slave-girl, regarding 'her' Mistress within. The Latin text of *Carmen* 67: 19-22 reads:

> *primum igitur virgo quod fertur tradita nobis*
> *falsum est non illam vir prior attigerat*
> *languidior tenera cui pendens sicula beta*
> *numquam se mediam sustulit ad tunicam*

Because Skinner (2003, p. 47) is discussing the unusual placement of the anti-sentimental 67 between two song-poems each of which extols a wife of unblemished virtue, she does not attempt to 'commit poetry', but instead presents a prose translation that is perfectly literal:

To begin with, then, that it's said a virgin was given to us
– that's untrue. Her first husband (whose dirk, hanging
limper than a young beet, never raised itself to mid-tunic)
wouldn't have touched her {alternatively: her husband
wouldn't have touched her first, or beforehand} ...

Skinner presents both senses of *prior* <previous *or* previous-
ly>; thus, "Her *first* husband ..." or "wouldn't have touched
her *first*", because the matter remains unsettled among scholars, and neither reading alters her explanation for 67's placement in the corpus.

Frank Olin Copley (1957, p. 84) translates this passage:

Well, first, they say we got a virgin bride:
no sir; her husband didn't get her first –
that languid sickly good-for-nothing lump,
he'd never make the grade – not half-way up.

Peter Whigham (1966, p. 168):

Then listen. The virgin lifted
    across this threshold was
bogus, the groom not the first to
    finger her, and his short
sword hung like a strip of limp beet
    between his legs, never
cocked navelwards ...

Jacob Rabinowitz (1991, p. 22):

Well, for a start, that "virgin bride" of Caecilius's was
    already married once.
– Not that her first husband ever touched her –
his weak little prick dangled like a rotten carrot.
It never raised its head belt high.

David Mulroy (2002, p 81):

For starters, the statement is wrong that a virgin moved in.
    It is true that her previous husband
had a dagger that dangled, a flabby beet, that never
    raised a tent in his tunic.

For Copley, Catullus let poetry "speak as other people spoke" (1957, p. xii). Thus, Copley's translation is as straightforward and sinewy as a poem by Carl Sandberg.

Rabinowitz's preface (pp. v-vii) leaves little doubt that *his* Catullus is a precursor of Allen Ginsberg, whose blurb on the back cover of Rabinowitz's book, "the most readable I know", suggests Ginsberg does not object to the implied comparison.

Mulroy's vocal style here is pulp fiction set to verse – not inappropriately so in a poem about a woman, her lovers, her cuckolded husband's lack of virility, and a lawsuit arising from her scandalous pregnancy.

Whigham has a style reminiscent of John Updike's verse (as well as his prose).

(Disclosure: *My* Catullus is forever Elvis-in-a-toga; *see* pp. 9-10 below.)

Note that two translators (Rabinowitz and Mulroy) each posit a second husband, while the other two (Copley and Whigham) make-do with merely one. Scholars seem evenly split on this issue (*see* Skinner 2003, p. 203, n. 49). Copley and Whigham thus avoid adoption of, or addition to, one of an array of already proposed 'back stories', without which the two-husband reading does not make sense within the context of the rest of 67. But, this poem contains no evidence of any of these proposed back stories, and their myriad complications are entirely inconsistent with the poem's obvious purpose as light, gossipy entertainment. Unsurprisingly, none of these scenarios has won wide acceptance. And yet, this 'ghost character' of a second husband lives on (*see* Giuseppe Giangrande, pp. 43-44 below).

Mulroy and Whigham indent alternating lines, in accord with the original's metric scheme of elegiac couplets (in which a metrically more emphatic line is followed by one that is less so). Mulroy (pp. xxxiii – xxxix) explains the metrical schemes of his own that he uses in translating the metrical patterns Catullus commonly uses, but does not provide his specific scheme for metricizing Catullus's infrequent employment of elegiac couplets.

Words and phrases from the Latin text, along with their literal English meaning <in brackets>, are followed by their translation by each author, and then commentary:

primum <first> *igitur* <(adverbial conjunction)>. Copley's "Well, first" is the only one of the four to render *primum* as "first". All but Whigham, though, aptly imply there is more to come. However, Rabinowitz's "for a start" and Mulroy's "for starters" are less in keeping than Copley with the Door's rhetorical pretensions. Whigham, instead, introduces the first of his 'novations': "Then listen."

fertur <it's said> is singular and passive. Copley's "they say" is plural and active, but it does imply that what follows is only rumor. Mulroy's "the statement" is a paraphrase, but also implies rumor. Rabinowitz and Whigham omit it – regrettably so, each in its own way.

virgo quod ... tradita nobis <that a virgin having been conveyed to us>:

Copley's "we got a virgin bride" would be more apropos were the Door speaking with one of her sister ancillaries. Here, however, the Door is employing rhetorical flourishes in order to convince an unnamed Interlocutor that she is superior to her Mistress's rumored activities.

Rabinowitz's "that 'virgin bride' of Caecilius's" tilts the table in favor of the two-husband reading by naming the Caecilius of 67:9 as a *second* husband. Indeed, "Caecilius" *is* the name of the (one and only) husband. But, as shall be seen (pp. 96-97 and n. 110 below), the husband is actually a familial relation of the "Caecilius" the Door now serves.

None of the four reflects that *tradita* <conveyed, *eg,* property}> in 67:19 mirrors *tradita* in 67:9, drawing a parallel between the conveyance of a residential property and that of a wife from her father to her groom. By rendering *tradita* as active rather than passive, Mulroy's "that a virgin moved in" transfers agency from her father and the groom to the bride herself.

Rabinowitz's "of Caecilius's" and Whigham's "lifted across this threshold" are also novations. Rabonowitz, as noted, wants to stack the deck in favor of a second husband. Whigham seems intent on 'improving' upon Catullus's verse.

falsum est <is a falsehood>: Copley's "no sir" is weaker than Mulroy's "is wrong". Rabinowitz further tilts the table with "was already married once". Unlike the other three, who correctly assert or imply that it is the bride's *repute* of maidenhood that is in error, Whigham, having omitted any form of "it's said", instead declares the wife herself "was bogus", though, as shall soon be seen, if anyone is "bogus", it is surely her groom.

non illam vir prior attigerit <not that the husband *could/ would* have touched her previously>:

Copley's "her husband didn't get her first" dispenses with the Door's attempt to put the matter somewhat more delicately.

Rabinowitz's "not that her first husband ever touched her", again, reads *prior* as "previous" instead of "previous*ly*".

Mulroy's "It is true that her previous husband" ignores the tactile *attigerit* <could/would have touched> in favor of emphasizing a second-husband reading.

Whigham's "the groom not the first to finger her", like Copley's rendering, ignores the subjunctive mood of *attigerit*, and in so doing implies that the husband, though not *first* to do so, does subsequently enjoy conjugal relations with his wife – yet the Door emphatically asserts its impossibility in the two lines that follow (as both translators recognize). However, Whigham nicely captures the sense of *attingere* as to touch with a finger.

languidior tenera cui pendens sicula beta <whose little dagger dangling more languidly than a tender beet>:

Copley's "that languid sickly good-for-nothing lump" apparently puns on *sicula* <little dagger> as "sickly". A *beta* <beet>, *tenera* <tender> or otherwise, is not a metaphor modern readers commonly associate with limpness, so improvisation is not unwarranted: Copley's "lump" is playfully one-letter different from "limp". *[P]endens* <dangling> does suggest "good-for-nothing" in this context.

Rabinowitz's "his weak little prick dangled like a rotten carrot" substitutes "little prick" for "little dagger". Though Catullus does bear some resemblance to the Beat Poets, the *Door* does not. Had she intended vulgarity rather than euphemism, the Door could have said *mentula*, which scans metrically with *sicula*. (Kudos to Skinner for "dirk", which in a single monosyllable conveys both the notion of small, and alliterates with an apropos slang word.) "[C]arrot" does improve on "beet" for modern readers, but "rotten" is almost an antonym of *tenera* <tender, hence young>.

Mulroy's "had a dagger that dangled, a flabby beet" nicely renders the first line of an elegiac couplet, with its greater density of emphasized syllables.

Whigham's "his short sword hung like a limp beet" is very close to literal, but "between his legs" is another novation. (Where else *would* a 'dirk' be *dangling?*)

Finally, *numquam se mediam sustulit ad tunicam* <never raised itself up to mid-tunic>: Tunics are not the typical attire of today's readers. Improvisation in translation of Catullus's metaphor for the husband's (rumored) erectile dysfunction is understandable, perhaps preferable.

But, Copley's "he'd never make the grade – not half-way up" disappoints in more than one respect. *[S]ustulit* <it raised up> is indicative, not subjunctive; and, *se* <itself> refers to the little dagger, not to the husband. Therefore, *numquam ... sustulit* ought be "never raised itself up". *[M]ediam ... tunicam* <mid-tunic> is an original metaphor that evokes a striking visual image. "[M]ake the grade – not half-way up" is an abstract cliché from academe trailed by an afterthought.

Rabinowitz's "It never raised its head belt-high" is spot-on.

Mulroy's "that never raised a tent in his tunic" is delightfully visual and alliterative.

Whigham's "never cocked navelward" is quite clever, though "*half*-cocked" would better capture *mediam*.

My own technique is to first puzzle through the syntax, grammar, and vocabulary until I am relatively confident that I have ascertained a line or phrase's literal meaning. Then, I attempt to respond to it in the way that jazz saxophonists Sonny Rollins and Sonny Stitt might exchange licks <u>bit.ly/qJAp32</u>:

> Well then ... *first* of all: The 'virgin' brought us
>   was a *fraudulent conveyance!*
> (Not that the groom *could have* probed her beforehand,
> he who, *little* dagger drooping limper than the letter *lambda,*
> never got it up to half-mast!)

Italicization has been added to indicate (what I imagine would be) the Door's vocal emphasis. The last three lines are surrounded by parentheses to suggest the Door's uttering these naughty details *sotto voce.* "[U]s" accurately reflects *nobis* as an indirect object. "[C]onveyance" preserves the sense of a property transfer (cf. n. 112 below). "*[C]ould have*" acknowledges that *attigerit* is subjunctive. "[B]eforehand" has been appropriated from Skinner because "-hand" hints at the tactile. And, "probed" is homage to Whigham's "fingered".

"[T]he letter *lambda*" is a novation of my own – a visual pun (λ) alluding to an alternative meaning of *beta* as the second letter of the Greek alphabet (β). "[N]ever got it up to half-mast" is as clichéd as Copley's metaphor, but is at least visual and reflects *mediam's* sense of half-ness.

The foregoing suggests two takeaways for students and other readers alike. First: the further a translation travels from literalness, the more it is likely the translation introduces elements contrary to the original poet's intended meaning. Second: Do not place great confidence in *someone else's* translation of Catullus.

Table of Contents

Dramatis Personae

Clodia Metelli/**Lesbia** (*nee* Claudia Pulchra Prima) – poet, playwright, patroness, and woman at the center of the most notorious scandal of the ancient Roman Republic.

Gaius Valerius **Catullus** – greatest love poet of ancient Rome; unable to stop loving **Clodia** even after he grows to hate her.

Marcus Tullius **Cicero** – Rome's greatest orator, attorney, and prose writer; Consul of the Roman Empire, 63 BCE; verbally excoriates **Clodia** during **Caelius's** trial for attempting to poison her.

Marcus **Caelius** Rufus – protégé of **Cicero** and boyhood friend of **Catullus** who replaces him in **Clodia's** affections.

Quintus Caecilius Metellus **Celer** – military commander; Consul of the Roman Empire, 60 BCE; **Clodia's** cuckold who dies mysteriously when her romance with **Caelius** gets underway.

Publius **Clodius** (*nee* Claudius) Pulcher – radical demagogue; **Clodia's** little brother, with whom she has enjoyed a 'special relationship' since their youth.

Caius Iulius **Caesar** – Pontifex Maximus (Supreme Pontiff) in 62 BCE; eventual Dictator of the Roman Empire (49 – 44 BCE).

Marcus Licinius **Crassus** – Richest man in Rome; **Caelius's** other mentor; **Pompey's** rival for military glory.

Pompey ("the Great") – military commander seeking to duplicate conquests of Alexander the Great; erstwhile ally of **Cicero**.

Ptolemy Auletes – Grecian King of Egypt for some 20 years.

Cleopatra – daughter of **Ptolemy**; last Pharaoh of Egypt; consort of **Caesar**, later **Mark Antony**, with whom she seeks conquest of the Roman Empire.

Mark Antony – attempts to succeed **Caesar**; orders assassination of one of his chief obstacles: **Cicero**.

Caecilius (II) – apparently a relative of **Celer** (Caecilius I) who inherits **Celer's** home in Verona in consequence of Clodia's failure to produce a male heir.

Part I: The Popcorn and Candy

The stuff of history, perhaps, but also of Hollywood.
(Julia Dyson Hejduk)

In the waning decades of the Dark Ages, like a candle long hidden under a bushel, there comes to light what is the now lost 'grandparent' (its two immediate 'progeny' also now lost) of the three oldest manuscripts of the surviving Catullan corpus. By so slender a thread has the work of one of antiquity's greatest and most influential poets survived to the present day.

Since that time what is now enumerated *Carmen* 67, sometimes called "The Door", has been read as a work-apart from the rest of Catullus's song-poems. It is universally understood to be wicked gossip circulating in Catullus's day; but, to my knowledge, no sustained attempt has been made to name the subjects of this gossip – other than the tall temperamental philanderer of the final lines. And, none of the conjectures as to *his* identity have found widespread acceptance.

This monograph presents a reading of *Carmen* 67 that is unique in several respects: 1) the major characters are all identified (as personages well-known to Catullus's circle);[3] 2) song-poem 67 is integrated into the other 'Lesbia poems'; 3) 67's allusions to both *Carmen* 35 ("Summon Caecilius") and Cicero's *Pro Caelio* are demonstrated (thereby making the identification of the pseudonymous "Lesbia" as Clodia Metelli more apparent yet); 4) TW Hillard's hypothesis regarding Celer's paternity is confirmed; 5) 67's 'Cornelius connection' to song-poems 1 and 102 is drawn; 6) the several peculiarities of the poem-within-a-poem (lines 32-34) are explained; and 7) with as much clarity as 67's inherent allusiveness will allow, the *real* reason Clodia brings a prosecution against her ex-lover, Marcus Caelius Rufus, is revealed.

Classicist Gennaro Perrotta writes: *Il carme 67 è, fra tutte le poesie di Catullo, forse la più difficile a interpretarsi* <*Carmen* 67 is, among all the poems of Catullus, perhaps the most difficult to interpret>. Wilhelm Kroll concludes his analysis of 67 with this wistful reflection: *Und nun bin ich neugierig, was der nächste Erklärer aus dem Gedichte machen wird* <But now I am curious what the next interpreter will make of this poem>. (Philip Levine, p. 62, n. 1-2)

It is the thesis of this monograph that the reading of Catullus's *Carmen* 67 xrl.us/bmfb4b that is most consistent with what is already believed by most commentators about Catullus and his world, as well as with the plain meaning of the text itself, can be summarized in a 3½-word sentence: *It's about Clodia.*

The Solution in Brief

Clodia Metelli (*nee* Claudia Pulchra Prima <Claudia the Beautiful I>) is a Roman aristocrat, poetess, playwright, and patroness of young men of various talents. To place her in time: She is likely just a few years younger than Julius Caesar.[4]

In her late 30s, while still married to the military commander Quintus Caecilius Metellus ("Swifty") Celer (ultimately a Roman Consul in 60 BCE, making Clodia in effect First Lady of the Roman Empire), she commences a love affair with the wildly mercurial "New Poet" Gaius Valerius ("the Puppy") Catullus, then in his early 20s.[5] Within a few years, though, she begins a liaison with Catullus's yet-younger boyhood friend, Marcus Caelius ("Rusty") Rufus, a tall dashing playboy and rising star in Roman politics.[6]

A few years subsequent (56 BCE), Clodia is in the open court of the Roman Forum accusing Caelius of attempting to poison her. The great lawyer/statesman Marcus Tullius ("Chick-Pea") Cicero,[7] in defending his wayward former understudy Caelius, attacks Clodia's credibility as a witness by retailing what seems like every bit of available gossip about Clodia's energetic libido.

Carmen 67 might well be entitled "And *That's* Not *All!*" Unsure himself what to believe, with gleeful malice Catullus's song-poem puts in the 'mouth' of a talkative front door (of Clodia's original marital home in Catullus's native Verona) the shocking slave-girl gossip emanating from within, both regarding the true nature of Clodia's marriage to Celer the cuckolded Consul, and the real reason Clodia has accused Caelius of trying to poison her.

2

Historical Context of Catullus's *Carmen* 67

Clodia – a woman not only noble, *but indeed truly* newsworthy!
(Marcus Tullius Cicero)

Rome, a former Tuscan farming and trading colony, establishes a Republican form of government around the time the already ancient city-state of Athens adopts certain institutions of Democracy (*c.* 508 BCE). In the early years of the 1st century BCE, Athens becomes a colony of Rome. But, Rome's Republican institutions, though they have been modified many times along the way, are increasingly dysfunctional.[8]

A sense is in the air that control of Western history's most fabled and fabulous empire – its expansion now rapidly accelerating – is 'up for grabs'.

A Controversial Woman

Clodia Metelli's lineage is comparable to that of a member of the current British Royal family:

> By the reckoning of the imperial biographer Suetonius, the patrician Claudii amassed during the lifetime of the Republic a total of twenty-eight consulships, five dictatorships, seven censorships, six triumphs, and two ovations.[9]

Wiseman (1987, p. 20) summarizes:

> [M]ulier nobilis [<noblewoman>] is putting it mildly: This daughter of the patrician Claudii was not merely a member of an ornamental social élite, but at the heart of the ruling class of the Roman Republic.

In addition to her activities in the literary and performing arts, Clodia is involved in populist politics, through promoting the career of her youngest brother, Publius Clodius ("Pretty-Boy") Pulcher, an effete demagogue who is not above employing his mob of plebeian followers to influence political outcomes.

To advance his career as a populist opponent of the Republican old guard, her brother at some point changes his *nomen* <clan name> from the loftily aristocratic "Claudius" to the more plebeian-friendly "Clodius". She likewise changes the name by which she is known from "Claudia" to "Clodia".

Clodia is also the object of a lifelong obsession of the greatest (male) love poet of Western literature, the emotionally volatile Catullus. And, during the final decades of his life, the Golden Age of Roman literature's greatest writer of prose, the conservative stalwart Cicero, also, is preoccupied with Clodia – in his censorious (and envious) fashion.[10]

Even by the standards of ancient Rome, Clodia is controversial; and the controversy surrounding Clodia continues to the present day.[11] Marilyn Berglund Skinner, the leading authority on Clodia, makes the following acute observations, drawn from Cicero's private correspondence:

> Cicero implicitly attests to her reliability and her diplomatic skills [1983, p. 278]; Clodius's remark indicates that he regarded his sister as a valuable political asset and flaunted her as such before his rivals [p. 279]; she took an independent stand, incurring public disapproval by championing her brother against her husband to the detriment of the conjugal bond [p. 280]; she has become a member of [Clodius's] circle of confidants [p. 280]; her earlier championship of Clodius notwithstanding, she was not then, and perhaps never was, his docile tool, but was willing to act autonomously in pursuit of her own private interests [p. 281]; what in fact seems to distinguish her from other women of her time, was her enterprise in face-to-face negotiations, coupled with a marked tendency toward personal autonomy [p. 285]; she chooses to remain single after her spouse's death, moves confidently in society, administers several estates – a house on the Palatine, her river property, a villa at Solonium, probably another at Baiae – and, in short, functions well in a man's world [p. 285].

There is no inconsistency, in theory or in practice, between the foregoing description of Clodia deduced by Skinner, and the accounts of Catullus and Cicero (in the latter's private correspondence as well as in *Pro Caelio*) of the sensational aspects of Clodia's behavior. Skinner's comment that "it is probable we will never recover the exact truth" (p. 285) of

Clodia's intimate life (and that of other ancient Roman women) is undeniable. However, one of Skinner's concluding remarks has not been received by this reader without (qualified) skepticism: "It is hard to think of her as the victim of unruly passions; she seems, on the contrary, firmly in control of her own life" (p. 287).

It would require several volumes to describe in detail the exact truth about a great many public figures of recent decades, in politics and in other realms, in the US and elsewhere, who have executed their professional responsibilities at a very high level of competence, yet have behaved quite irresponsibly in their private lives. Indeed, some have acted with alarming recklessness.[12]

Clodia's brother Clodius's power and efficacy as a Tribune of the People (58 BCE) turns out to have been far from unimpressive. (*See* W Jeffrey Tatum generally.) But, few would suggest Clodius's private conduct was without its share of impropriety. The public achievements of Caesar and Pompey are far greater still, yet this fact alone does not argue against their possessing scandalous private foibles.

Those scholars who reason that charges of sexual misconduct, particularly incest, in ancient Roman political invective are so prevalent as to cast doubt upon them, seem to be arguing that there is *too much* smoke for there to be fire. Yet, no one argues that the frequency of charges of financial corruption, then or now, is reason for skepticism as to their truth. Indeed, in the contemporary context, though charges of sexual misconduct against public figures are occasionally inaccurate, for the most part they are eventually confirmed.

But, Skinner is likely correct in concluding that, based upon the extant record, Clodia does not seem to be the "victim" of anyone or anything. On the contrary, it appears that her husband Celer the Consul and military commander, Catullus the New Poet, the tall charismatic Caelius, and Cicero the Consul and great orator, in one way or another, are *her* victims.

At all events, the irreducible fact is that however much either or both of Cicero and Catullus may be exaggerating the sensational elements of Clodia's conduct, no other woman of the

ancient world has inspired so much rousing prose and arou-
sing poetry – by two authors who know her *personally.*

Catullus begins *Carmen* 5 xrl.us/bmfftg:

> *vivamus mea lesbia atque amemus*
> *rumoresque senum severiorum*
> *omnes unius aestimemus assis ...* (1-3)

> Let's live and let's love, my *Lesbia,*
> and prize the prattle of all the
> prudish prunes at a *penny!* ...

(Alas, Catullus: Be careful what you wish for.)

How Ingrate Thou Art

Skinner's view that Clodia has been poorly served by more
traditional scholars is not without warrant: Catullus's epistola-
ry *Carmen* 49 xrl.us/bmfcdt expresses such exaggerated
praise of Cicero that some critics have read into it sarcastic
intent. The poet does not explicitly state the reason for his
gratitude, but *Carmen* 49 contains clear references to *Carmen* 36 xrl.us/bmfhyh, which in turn is about *mea puella*
<my Mistress, *ie,* Clodia> (36:2). At 36:6, Catullus smirks
that Clodia has scorned him as *pessimi poetae* <the *worst*
poet *ever*> (perhaps after she reads 67). In 49, after referring
to himself twice as *pessimus omnium poeta* <the worst poet of
all> (49:5-6), Catullus concludes by hailing Cicero as *tanto ...
/ tu quanto optimus omnium patronus* <by equal measure, you
are the best lawyer of *all* [the defendants]> (36:5-6), cheekily
implying a certain moral equivalence with Cicero's characterization of Clodia as *amicam omnium* <a 'friend' of *all* the
men> (*Pro Caelio* 32; *see* n. 51 below).

In making his case that song-poem 49 is *not* sincerely intended, the influential scholar Kenneth Quinn asks rhetorically (1972b, p. 198; and again, 1973, p. 234):

> But would [Catullus] *really* feel grateful? Could the Les-
> bia poems survive Cicero's brilliant witty demonstration
> that falling in love with Clodia stamped you as the dupe
> of a worthless nymphomaniac? [Emphasis in the 1973
> version. Quoted, approvingly, by Fredricksmeyer, p. 269.]

Similarly, Quinn (1972b, p. 107): "... the sordid reality of [Lesbia's] worthlessness."

(Note to younger readers: "nymphomaniac" is an anachronistic pseudo-medical term for a woman whom the {putative} diagnostician fears is having much more fun than the diagnostician. The modern term is "slut", which is, approvingly, applied to "any gender" xrl.us/bmda89.)

Quinn's question might more tellingly be reversed: Would the Lesbia song-poems have survived were *not* Catullus Clodia's fool?[13]

With regards to feelings of gratitude, it seems to this reader that not only Catullus, but subsequent scholars a not insignificant portion of whose career has been predicated upon commenting about her, should all be grateful to Clodia that she is "Lesbia", rather than, say, the angelic Queen Berenice of *Carmen* 66 xrl.us/bmfcij.

Who's Sorry Now?[14]

Would Catullus *not* really feel grateful to Cicero for being the ringmaster of a veritable Roman Circus in which the song-poet's former lover, and his boyhood friend who won her away, make spectacles of themselves in front of a holiday crowd assembled in the Roman Forum? Would he not be especially grateful to Cicero for putting some of Clodia's more scandalous activities onto the public record? Beside whatever *Schadenfreud* it may afford Catullus, it also liberates him, now that Clodia has been publicly exposed by Cicero, to be much more candid in his own exposés about "Lesbia" (*eg*, *Carmen* 67).

On the subject of gratitude, Arthur Symon concludes his poem "Lesbia in Old Age" with Lesbia wearily lamenting: "Can not Catullus pity me / Although my name upon his scroll / Has brought him immortality?" (Wiseman 1987, p. 227). Setting aside the evidence that Catullus, not Clodia, seeks pity, how "worthless" could Clodia be, in light of her providing Catullus with the literary immortality he prays for in concluding the very first poem of the collection (1:9-10)? By contrast, as Whigham (p. 25) notes of New Poets other than Catullus: "The surviving fragments of the works of Calvus,

Cinna, Cornificius, Bibaculus, and Ticidas occupy barely three pages of print."

Surely, none of us (certainly not myself) would want to be forever tarred by our most awkward turn of phrase, particularly if viewed through a lens directed at it some four decades later. As with many of us, Quinn's perspective may have evolved since the quoted passages are first published.

Nevertheless, Skinner presumably is a student at that time (the early 1970s). In such a context, it is not surprising that she, and a number of other scholars from that era right up to the present, would feel strongly that an injustice has been done to historical truth, and thus would be energized to set the record straight.

My own thoughts are that under current cultural norms there is no need to 'domesticate' Clodia/Lesbia. It is highly likely that she is not greatly different from the descriptions provided by traditional commentators on the one hand, and that Skinner and like-minded scholars provide on the other: A very gifted, independent, and wealthy noblewoman proud to be conducting her life according to her own interests and needs – just as are the men around her.

The pursuit of truth is often an ongoing process of iteration, rather than a one-time triangulation.

Sapphica Puella

Plato is reported to have deemed Sappho "the 10th Muse". Clodia is Catullus's Sappho, which is implicit in his term of endearment for her, "Lesbia" (Sappho is born on the Aegean island of Lesbos late in the 7th Century BCE, and that locale has been associated with her ever since[15]). In my reading, he makes this analogy explicit in *Carmen* 35:16-17 – *sapphica puella / musa doctior* <Sapphic Mistress more knowing than a Muse> (*see* pp. 69-75 below).

Peering between the lines of *Pro Caelio*, and drawing a plausible inference from an observation of Roland Gregory Austin (*see* n. 4 below), it seems to this reader that Clodia's role as 'Great Mother' (cf. *Carmina* 35 and 63) to the New Poets parallels Sappho's role as head of a finishing school for girls.

Puppy Love

When probably in her late 30s, Clodia begins a liaison with Catullus, who is likely yet in his early 20s – though she is still in an arranged marriage (Skinner 2010, p. 79) with the stuffy (and, Catullus gloatingly insists, impotent and sterile[16]) military commander and eventual Roman Consul, Metellus Celer. Hence, she is known to history as "Clodia Metelli".

Deliriously happy, Catullus writes love poems to Clodia so touching that almost two millennia later British Poet Laureate Alfred Lord Tennyson deems Catullus "the tenderest poet".

Quinn (1973, p. xii) observes:

> [I]n antiquity Catullus was among the most read and the most talked about of Roman poets. That Virgil had studied the poems as one craftsman studies the work of another is clear ...

Shakespeare's sonnets are hailed by more than one contemporaneous critic as being on par with Catullus's lyric poems.[17]

But, Clodia eventually shares her charms with a rising star in Rome's political ferment, Marcus Caelius Rufus, a younger boyhood friend of Catullus (*Carmen* 100 xrl.us/bmfbyy).[18]

The Birth of the Blues

Catullus, devastated by this dual betrayal, reacts by inventing the Blues, the five-word premise of which is of course: *My baby done left me.*

Surely, many poets prior to Catullus have written poems about romantic heartbreak. The most famous of them is the aforementioned Sappho; and Clodia/Lesbia is the embodiment of Sappho's spirit for her adoring puppy.[19] By analogy, in the modern era Elvis is not the first to sing the Blues with a rockin' beat; but, he is nonetheless the first *Rocker*, in that this becomes his full-time persona. It is in this sense that Catullus is the first Blues singer. Not merely the theme for which he is most known, my-baby-done-left-me (and-then-my-brother-died) is Catullus's *identity*.

Moreover, based upon the extant body of ancient poetry, it appears it is Catullus who invents the motif of the Slave of

Love, which so many poets and popular entertainers have subsequently emulated. Unlike later poets, Catullus does not explicitly refer to himself as his beloved's slave, but rather to Lesbia as his *Domina* <slave-mistress> (*Carmen* 68B:68,156 xrl.us/bmhhd2), during an era, it should be recalled, when slaves are *slaves*.[20]

The parallel ought not be overdrawn. Skinner (1993, p. 62):

> Of course, Catullus was never a professional entertainer: his station as *domi nobilis* [<from a noble home>], scion of one of the principal families of Verona, precludes that supposition.

To be sure, Catullus's parents host the likes of Caesar at their home (see n. 76 below). Elvis's parents are unable to afford even a simple marker to indicate where Elvis's stillborn twin brother, Jesse, is buried.[21] Catullus's target audience, as well as his social circle, are a highly cultured elite. Elvis is immediately accessible to every listener.

However, the analogy does not completely miss its mark. Skinner (*ibid*), enthusiastically recommending classroom recital of certain song-poems of Catullus (including the notorious *Carmen* 16 xrl.us/bmhhe7),[22] observes:

> In his 1983 study *L'élégie érotique romaine*, Veyne envisioned a Catullus perceived by listeners "as we ourselves perceive popular singers," one who "took his own name, Catullus, as his stage name" (cited from Pellauer's English translation ...).

As with Elvis, so with Catullus: There had been no one like him before; and afterward, as has been said of Elvis, "Everybody else is an imitator ... "[23]

The common essence, in addition to their revolutionary originality, is that both Catullus and Elvis are spiritual sons of Sappho who could express their pained longing for a woman as a woman might.[24] *In a sense, Catullus is the 'male Sappho'; and Elvis is the 'American Catullus'.* Thus, thousands of years later, Sappho and Catullus are still being read and heard; it is not unlikely that thousands of years hence, the work of all three will still have much of its original impact.[25]

The Tall Temperamental Russet-Haired Man

Though Caelius's immediate family may have been based in Teramo, near the Adriatic Coast of Central Italy,[26] he has spent at least some portion of his youth as the boyhood friend of Catullus in the latter's hometown of Verona.[27]

Upon arrival in Rome, Caelius is placed under the tutelage of both Cicero and Marcus Licinius ("the Crass") Crassus (Wiseman 1987, p. 62). Crassus is reputedly the richest man in the Western world of the day, and in 59 BCE will become a member, along with Caesar and Pompey the Great, of an unofficial "1ˢᵗ Triumvirate" <three-man junta> who, in conjunction with a number of less important figures, rule Rome for a time as a shadow government (Hejduk, p. 239).

After his training, Caelius sets out on his own, flirting with the radical populist Catiline. In 63 BCE, having failed at electoral politics, Catiline conspires to kill Cicero (then Consul of Rome), along with a number of other Senators, and thus seize control of the Roman Empire. The coup attempt fails. Caelius (and, interestingly, Crassus) soon leave Rome for two years or so. By contrast, Clodius is a conspicuous ally of Cicero in his hour of mortal peril.[28]

Pulchellus Puer <*Little Pretty-Boy Clodius*>[29]

In December of the following year, Clodius, *en femme* as a lute-playing slave-girl (perhaps with Clodia's assistance – after all, she is a playwright[30]), gains admittance to the annual women-only sacred rites to the *Dea Bona* <Good Goddess>, her actual name too holy to reveal (to men).[31]

The ceremony is attended by Roman women of the highest social status, and presided over by the Vestal Virgins, themselves Roman women of high rank. That year the rituals are performed in the residence of the *Pontifex Maximus* <Supreme Pontiff> (at the time, Caesar). Plutarch relates that Clodius goes to the rites seeking an assignation with Pompeia, sister of Pompey the Great and current wife of Caesar, who of course would not be present at an all-women gathering.

However, perhaps Clodius does not need a reason for being his merry self – he just needs an occasion. With obvious relish, Cicero later describes Clodius's 'fashion statement' of that evening:

> *clodius a crocota a mitra a muliebribus soleis purpureis-*
> *que fasceolis a strophio a psalterio a flagitio a stupro est*
> *factus repente popularis nisi eum mulieres exornatum ita*
> *deprendissent nisi ex eo loco quo eum adire fas non fuerat*
> *ancillarum beneficio emissus esset populari homine popu-*
> *lus romanus res publica cive tali careret hanc ob amenti-*
> *am in discordiis nostris de quibus ipsis his prodigiis recen-*
> *tibus a dis immortalibus admonemur arreptus est unus ex*
> *patriciis cui tribuno plebis* (*Haruspicum Responsis* 44 <u>xrl.u</u>
> <u>s/bign8g</u>)

Clodius, from a saffron chemise, from a tiara, from wo-men's slippers with lavender bows, from a bustier, from singing with lyre, from shamelessness, from strumpetry, is suddenly made into a '*man* of the people'! The women having caught him thus attired, if he hadn't fled that lo-cation he was forbidden to enter – able to escape through beneficence afforded by slave-girls – the Roman people would have been spared this populist '*man* of the people', and the Republic this 'public *servant*'!

Caesar is not present, of course. But Caesar's mother, Aurel-ia, is. She has a slave-girl of her own ask Clodius why 'she' is looking for Aurelia's daughter-in-law, Pompeia. The mascu-line timbre of Clodius's voice reveals his gender. Chaos erupts; he hides; he escapes; Rome is outraged.[32]

As a result, Clodius is prosecuted for *Incestus* <sacrilege> through *libera interpretatio* <liberal interpretation> of the legal prohibition against compromising the virtue of a Vestal Virgin (Tatum, p. 75). Technically, *Incestus* is not necessarily what it appears to be in English, but in this case Clodius's past incest with a sister (other than our Clodia) is also alleged – by her former husband, Lucius Licinius Lucullus.

Years earlier Clodius, feeling underappreciated, led a short-lived mutiny, costing Lucullus his military command (Green 2005, p. 284). Lucullus doubtlessly has not forgotten.

Caesar avoids testifying by pointing out that he was not there, and thus has no evidence to offer. He does divorce Pompeia, though, giving rise to the adage: Caesar's wife must be above *suspicion*.

Cicero, however, has evidence that squarely contradicts Clodius's alibi for the evening in question. The great orator and former Consul must now decide whether to proffer such evidence.

"The Savior of the Republic" [33]

Cicero is born in 106 BCE to modestly successful, though not noble, parentage in Arpino, some 70 miles east by southeast of Rome. Plutarch relates (*Cicero* 2.2 xrl.us/bmez3x):

> When he was of an age for taking lessons, his natural talent shone out clear and he won name and fame among the boys, so that their fathers used to visit the schools in order to see Cicero with their own eyes and observe the quickness and intelligence in his studies for which he was extolled, though the ruder ones among them were angry at their sons when they saw them walking with Cicero placed in their midst as a mark of honour.

Notwithstanding the prejudice of class-conscious patricians against this *novo homo* <newcomer> to Rome's political class, and though he has a relatively late start in his public life, by dint of talent and sheer hard work Cicero is able to win election to every important office in Rome – at the statutory minimum age – including a Consulship in 63 BCE.

Having reached the political pinnacle at age 43 (a Consulship in which, with the military assistance of Celer, the Catilinarian conspiracy is decisively defeated), Cicero suffers political and personal setbacks for much of the rest of his life. He makes compromises necessary to his political and personal survival along the way. But no one (save for the even more censorious Cato the Younger) struggles harder to prevent the Republic of Rome from transmogrifying into monarchy. In the end, both are on the losing side of history, and thereby lose their lives.

On the subject of *love*, Cicero is not restrained in expressing his disapproval:

sic igitur adfecto haec adhibenda curatio est ut et illud quod cupiat ostendatur quam leve quam contemnendum quam nihili sit omnino quam facile vel aliunde vel alio modo perfici vel omnino neglegi possit abducendus etiam est non numquam ad alia studia sollicitudines curas negotia loci denique mutatione tamquam aegroti non convalescentes saepe curandus est ..... maxume autem admonendus est quantus sit furor amoris omnibus enim ex animi perturbationibus est profecto nulla vehementior ut si iam ipsa illa accusare nolis stupra dico et corruptelas et adulteria incesta denique quorum omnium accusabilis est turpitudo sed ut haec omittas perturbatio ipsa mentis in amore foeda per se est (*Tusculanae Disputationes* 4.74-75 xrl. us/bme64t)

So, therefore, in attempting to hold forth a cure for him who may have this urge [love], it should be shown how inconsequential, how contemptible, how utterly nihilistic it be. How easily it could be achieved either from elsewhere, or in another manner – or be entirely *disregarded*. To wit, not infrequently, one might be directed to the distractions of other pastimes, or to diligence in business. Lastly, with a change of location – just as the cure of those still convalescing from infirmity is often effected.

.... *This above all:* However much be the *insanity* of love – indeed, of all the mental disturbances, none is more vehement, so at this point you would NOT want to go so far as to accuse love itself, I say, of strumpetry and corruption and adultery and, finally, incest, which of all accusations is *most* evil (but such you may *dis*regard) – the mental disturbance of love *itself* is filth *per se!*

Since Cicero views love as a mental illness, a gateway to sex crime, and, in its very essence, just plain dirty, it is safe to surmise that the 'chemistry' between himself and Clodia is not ideal. (For Cicero's {private} envy of Clodia's liberated lifestyle, *see* Wiseman's comment on p. 19 below.)

Though Cicero's accomplishments are many, his only permanent achievements are his writings (beside our calendar, ditto Caesar). Among these, over 900 letters survive (many more circulated in ancient times). In more than 800, Cicero is the sender; about half of these are to his friend and confidant Atticus (Shackleton Bailey, p. xi). The letters provide much of what is known of the watershed period of the ancient West: Rome's transformation from the Republic to the Principate.

Cicero does not expect his private correspondence to someday be made public; hence these letters provide a unique window for peering into an important historical figure's private thoughts. Shackleton Bailey (p. xii) notes: "Nothing comparable has survived out of the classical world." He provides an almost Zen-like summary of the great man (p. 5):

> Cicero the upright patriot (with human weaknesses) and Cicero the time-serving humbug are familiar figures. Neither convinces.

"A Woman Eager for Distinction"

Plutarch relates that Cicero's wife, Terentia, suspecting Clodia of wanting to replace Celer with Cicero, decisively influences Cicero to testify against Clodius in the *Dea Bona* trial. Skinner (2010, p. 9) remarks:

> [Plutarch] attributes Cicero's falling-out with [Clodia's] brother to the jealous suspicions of Cicero's wife, Terentia .... Patent inequalities in birth and wealth between Clodia's own husband, Celer, then governor of Cisalpine Gaul, and Cicero, then an ex-consul but still a small-town parvenu, make the story absurd. She would have nothing to gain from such a match.

And yet, as *Terentia* may have viewed the matter, from Clodia's perspective an alliance with the more malleable Cicero might succeed in neutralizing an influential opponent of Clodius's populist agenda, a goal Clodia has not achieved with her (politically) rigid husband, Celer. Plutarch does not write that Clodia is contemplating this option, but rather:

> Terentia thought [Clodia] to be desirous of marrying Cicero and to be contriving this with the aid of a certain Tullus; now, Tullus was a companion and an especial intimate of Cicero, and his constant visits and attentions to Clodia, who lived near by, made Terentia suspicious. [Perrin, *Plutarch: Parallel Lives – Cicero* 29.2 xrl.us/bmbv7j]

The reader may ask herself: Who would *not* be suspicious of Clodia's intentions regarding her significant other under like circumstances? Moreover, a bit further along in his narrative (30.4), Plutarch writes regarding Clodius's efforts to dissuade Cicero from joining Caesar's staff in Gaul:

> Clodius, perceiving that Cicero would thus escape his tribunician authority, professed to be inclinable to a reconciliation, laid the greatest fault upon Terentia, made always a favourable mention of him, and addressed him with kind expressions, as one who felt no hatred or ill-will, but who merely wished to urge his complaints in a moderate and friendly way.

It thus seems that when it is to his tactical advantage, Clodius himself is willing to go along with the Terentia-made-Cicero-do-it explanation.

The overarching theme of Plutarch's *Parallel Lives* is to demonstrate similarities between the respective characters of certain famous Romans with men Plutarch views as their Greek counterpart. Hence, Plutarch assigns the illustration of moral truths higher priority than literal truths. His larger point here, it seems, is that Terentia exercises a strong influence on Cicero's actions. Thus we find in Plutarch this startling revelation of the power that Terentia, apparently, exerts over Cicero in one of his most fateful decisions: Seeking the death penalty, without trial, for several Roman Senators engaged in Catiline's conspiracy against the Republic:

> For there was no likelihood, if [the conspirators] suffered less than death, they would be reconciled, but rather, adding new rage to their former wickness, they would rush into every kind of audacity, while [Cicero] himself, whose character for courage already did not stand very high with the multitude, would be thought guilty of the greatest cowardice and want of manliness.

Whilst Cicero was doubting what course to take, a portent happened to the women in their sacrificing. For on the altar, where the fire seemed wholly extinguished, a great and bright flame issued forth from the ashes of the burnt wood; at which others were affrighted, but the holy virgins [Vestal Virgins] called to Terentia, Cicero's wife, and bade her haste to her husband, and command him [*sic*] to execute what he had resolved for the good of his country, for the goddess had sent a great light to the increase of his safety and glory. Terentia, therefore, as she was otherwise in her own nature neither tender-hearted nor timorous, but a woman eager for distinction (who, as Cicero himself says, would rather thrust herself into his public affairs, than communicate her domestic matters to him), told him these things, and excited him against the conspirators. (Perrin, *Plutarch: Parallel Lives – Cicero* 19.5-20.2 xrl.us/bme4gw)

Hence, according to Plutarch's sources (which were more plentiful in his day than ours), the Vestal Virgins assume that Terentia (who is the wealthier and more socially prominent of the two when they marry) can bend Cicero to her will, even in deciding a life and death matter of the greatest political sensitivity.

It is worthy of note that notwithstanding her reputation for being inclined to "thrust herself into [Cicero's] public affairs", nary a word of personal scandal is attributed by the ancients to Terentia. By implication, regardless of the degree to which Clodia's political support of her brother's radical politics may be exacerbating the enmity of Cicero, and no doubt others of her brother's political opponents, it cannot completely explain why so much personal scandal attaches to Clodia, yet none attaches to Terentia.

Truth and Consequences

At Clodius's trial for *Incestus*, Cicero testifies that he spoke with the accused earlier on the day in question, thereby shredding Clodius's alibi that he was instead in Teramo – too far from Rome to attend the *Dea Bona* rites that evening. Caesar's mother, Aurelia, and sister Julia testify as eye witnesses to Clodius's having been at the ceremony. Lucullus's slaves testify to Clodius's trysts with the sister of Clodius who was formerly married to their master.

Nevertheless, Clodius wins acquittal (31-25) from a jury intimidated by a crowd of Clodius's plebeian supporters and, according to Cicero, bribed with more than money.[34] Clodius had stood by Cicero during the Catilinarian conspiracy to overthrow the Republic – and to kill Cicero in the process. As events will prove, Hades hath no fury like Clodius – and Clodia – scorned.

The Apprentice Bests the Master

In 59 BCE Caelius, having returned to Rome, brings a prosecution against Caius Antonius ("Half-Breed") Hybrida, the corrupt politician who was the upright Cicero's co-Consul in 63 BCE (Austin, p. vi). Cicero undertakes Antonius's defense, as a stain upon his former co-Consul's reputation would be a stain upon Cicero's. In his defense of Antonius, Cicero draws invidious contrasts with the strongmen rule of the Triumvirs, especially Caesar.[35] To Cicero's chagrin, Caelius wins the case.

Caelius is now Rome's man of the hour. Clodius arranges for Caelius to live in one of Clodius's apartments on the tony Palatine Hill – nearby Clodia's 'playhouse'.[36] Romance soon flourishes between Clodia and Caelius (much to Catullus's bitter disillusionment, as reflected in a number of his subsequent song-poems[37]).

The Gay Widow

Clodia's husband, Celer, as Consul in 60 BCE staunchly opposes Clodius's attempt to transfer to plebeian status in order to qualify for the formidable office of Tribune of the People (Skinner 2010, p. 85). Since the ancient purpose of the Tribunate has been to counterbalance patrician power, the aristocratic Clodius's plan is a mockery of the essence of this office. (It may be sometime in this period that Claudia and Claudius adopt the more plebeian-sounding names "Clodia" and "Clodius".)

While Consul, Celer publicly threatens to personally kill Clodius.[38] In March 59 BCE, just subsequent to his Consulship and while in Rome at home with Clodia on leave from his military command in Northern Italy, Celer, then only about 44 (and, according to Cicero, in fine form before the Senate a few days earlier), dies after a mysterious three-day illness – that seems a lot like poisoning. Coincidentally, Celer's untimely death makes marriage between Clodia and Caelius possible.

Choking back tears (perhaps sincerely felt), Cicero recalls:

> *vidi enim vidi et illum hausi dolorem vel acerbissimum in vita cum q metellus abstraheretur e sinu gremioque patriae cumque ille vir qui se natum huic imperio putavit tertio die post quam in curia quam in rostris quam in re publica floruisset integerrima aetate optimo habitu maximis viribus eriperetur indignissime bonis omnibus atque universae civitati* (*Pro Caelio* 59 xrl.us/bki59b)

Yes, I *saw!* I *saw* it, and I drank life's bitterest tears when the body and soul of Quintus Metellus [Celer] was draining away from the homeland – that man who always thought himself a Son of this Empire. The third day after he had flourished so in the Senate House, so on the Rostrum, so in public affairs, minimally touched by age, optimal in appearance, maximal in vigor, he had been ripped most undeservedly from all the best and brightest, as well as the citizenry as a whole!

A month after Celer's sudden demise, Clodia is hostessing a drunken orgy in her home on the Palatine (nearby Cicero's):

> *mihi exspectationem dedisti convivi istius ἀσελγοῦς sum in curiositate ὀξύπεινος sed tamen facile patior te id ad me συμπόσιον non scribere praesentem audire malo* (April 19, 59 BCE, *Atticus* 2.12.2 xrl.us/bifmj3)

[Atticus,] you have made me so curious about [Clodia's] orgy – I am starving for the dish! But, I can easily deal with your not writing about the *'vino conveno'* – I'd like to hear it in person!

Wiseman (1987, p. 43) comments about the letter as a whole: "[I]t is clear enough from Cicero's language that what he was dying to hear was not so much the political outlook as what went on at the sort of party he never got invited to himself."

Clodius Rising

Meanwhile, a much larger problem than not being on Clodia's 'A-list' is unfolding for Cicero. Conveniently for Clodia and Clodius, Celer's death removes a major obstacle to Clodius's sham 'adoption' by Fonteius, a 20-year-old plebeian.

Under Roman law and custom, the powerful post of Tribune of the People is virtually inviolable. Because of Cicero's attack on Caesar and Pompey while defending Antonius, and because, as a Tribune, Clodius would be positioned to intimidate their Republican foe, within hours of Antonius's conviction the two Triumvirs (ignoring legal anomalies of substance and process) allow Clodius to be formally adopted into a plebeian family.[39] Thus empowered to stand for office, Clodius wins election, becoming a Tribune of the People in 58 BCE.

Catiline's Revenge

As noted in the above discussion of Terentia, in the immediate wake of Catiline's coup attempt in 63 BCE, Cicero, with the Senate's consent (over the strong objection of the possibly complicit Caesar) executes several of the conspirators without trial – understandably, since jury verdicts could be bought, as would later occur in the trial of Clodius for *Incestus*. Even if convicted, the maximum statutory sentence for a Roman Senator is exile. As Plutarch points out, this would leave the conspirators free to continue their plotting.

By invoking Cicero's extra-judicial executions of Roman citizens, Clodius in the course of his 58 BCE Tribunate is able to have *ex post facto* laws adopted that, though facially neutral, are implicitly intended to drum Cicero out of Italy.

Cicero wants to stay and fight, and seeks support from the patricians on whose behalf he tirelessly has labored. Some of them would no doubt have perished had Catiline's coup attempt succeeded. Their advice to Cicero: Leave town. While in exile contemplating suicide, Cicero is deeply embittered by their failure to come to his aid.[40]

During Cicero's absence, Clodius's mob of followers burn to the ground Cicero's extravagantly expensive mansion on the Palatine, and Clodius pushes through legislation confiscating Cicero's other properties. Clodia harasses Cicero's wife and daughter, Terentia and Tullia (cf. Plutarch's explanation for Cicero's testimony against Clodius), who stay in Rome to plead on Cicero's behalf. Moreover, Clodia likely helps herself to the jewelry and other personalty of Terentia and Tullia.[41]

However, with the help of his friends and Clodius's enemies, after sixteen months in exile Cicero returns to Italy to cheering crowds. (*Atticus* 4.1.5 <u>xrl.us/bmfze4</u>)

Plus ça change ...

Wiseman (1987, pp. 1-14) explains that ancient Rome is "a world not ours". Thus, contemporary readers may find it difficult to comprehend the political currents of that time and place. However, Wiseman (pp. 54-62) concisely sets forth the complexities that lead to the trial of Caelius (and thus to Catullus's *Carmen* 67):

An escalation in food prices in Egypt, and heavy taxation to support a corrupt dictator and his family, leads to rioting in the streets of Egypt's capital, then Alexandria, eventually toppling the dictator's regime.

The dictator appeals to the Senate for support, emphasizing that he has been Rome's faithful ally for decades. The Senate dithers for a time, hoping the problem will go away. Doubling down, the dictator borrows heavily in order to make large scale 'campaign contributions' to Caesar and Pompey for distribution to other entrepreneurial Senators. The Egyptian dictator can repay the borrowed money only by levying higher taxes yet.

Senators who favor supporting the dictator's regime argue that not to support it would send the wrong signal to other allies. Opponents ask whether yet another war in that part of the world would be wise? Proponents counter that lenders might not be repaid by a new regime. Opponents answer that Rome does not need to be hated by the people of Egypt more than it already is.

A delegation representing the people of Alexandria is dispatched to plead with the Senate to not support the dictator. The eminence among the 100 diplomats is the philosopher Dio of Alexandria.

When the delegation arrives on the Italian mainland, in-place agents of the dictator foment riots and kindred disturbances that kill some of the diplomats, and terrorize the others into silence. The frightened Dio goes into hiding, but is soon fatally poisoned.

Then as now, the physical safety of foreign diplomats is sacrosanct under law. As with Clodius's penetration of the *Dea Bona* rites, the Senate cannot ignore a scandal of such dimension as the killing of an eminent envoy on Italian soil.

Back in Rome, Caelius is further vexing Cicero by preparing a second prosecution of Lucius Calpurnius ("the Beast") Bestia for political corruption, a man whom Cicero already has defended successfully against an earlier prosecution by Caelius.

Magnas Lites *<The Great Arguments>*

> *[T]he search for political motives and factors in the trial is condemned to a degree of speculation daunting even by the standards of classical scholarship.* (W Jeffrey Tatum)

Clodia and Clodius spring into action, using as their frontman an adopted son of Bestia, Lucius Sempronius Atratinus. The 17-year-old Atratinus, with trepidation, is trying his first case, hoping to derail a second prosecution of his father by bringing a prosecution against Caelius.

Although our only knowledge of the specific charges must be inferred from Cicero's rebuttal, *Pro Caelio* (which is not completely clear on the subject), the accusations against Caelius appear to be criminally culpable involvement with 1) the rioting in Naples attendant to the arrival of the Egyptian envoys, 2) associated violence at the nearby port of Pozzuoli, 3) an otherwise unexplained property dispute with one Palla, 4) the fatal poisoning of Dio, and, most sensationally, 5) attempting to poison Clodia (Austin, p. 152).

Charges 1, 2, and 4 constitute *Vis* <political violence>, a crime so serious that it is tried on the holiday of the Megalenses Games (which honor Goddess Cybele, the Great Mother), though other courts are closed for that occasion.

However, it is not Atratinus who speaks to these charges. Nor is it the third prosecution speaker, the elderly Lucius Herennius ("Baldy") Balbus. By inference from the defense's rebuttal, these two prosecutors focus almost entirely on Caelius's alleged moral failings, particularly sexual misbehavior, but also high-living that implies excessive debts that have thereby led to financial corruption.

In the course of censuring Caelius for his love affair with Clodia, Balbus does mention Clodia's allegation that Caelius has borrowed gold jewelry from her, under pretense of financing a spectacle to win popular support, but instead to fund *Vis* against the Alexandrian emissaries and the poisoning of Dio.

Yet, neither Atratinus nor Balbus address in any sustained manner the charges that Caelius had a role in the general violence against the Egyptian delegation, and specifically in the fatal poisoning of Dio. These charges are instead declaimed by the second of the three prosecutors, Clodia's brother Clodius.[42]

Witness for the Prosecution[43]

The climax of the prosecution's case is Clodia's testimony that Caelius attempted to poison her when she learned he had used her jewelry to fund *Vis,* rather than a public spectacle.

To review: Caelius has some degree of association with Catiline around the time of Catiline's attempt on Cicero's life. Caelius's successful prosecution of Cicero's former co-Consul, Antonius, a few years later is not only a blow to the (considerable) vanity of Caelius's former mentor; it also adds to an existing suspicion that Cicero and Antonius shared in the latter's financial exploitation of Macedonia during his governorship there.[44]

Caelius soon thereafter becomes romantically involved with Clodia, and is therefore almost surely allied politically with Clodius during this period. Hence, having earlier been in some way allied with a man plotting to kill Cicero, in more recent years Caelius has been aligned with two of Cicero's bitterest personal foes.

And now Caelius is preparing to prosecute a client of Cicero for a *second* time. As an obstacle to a second trial of Bestia, the prosecution of Caelius for *Vis*, even if unsuccessful, can only help Cicero. In light of the foregoing, it seems probable that Clodia and Clodius think Cicero to be the last orator in Rome willing to defend Caelius.

But, in the event, the flexible Cicero takes up the defense of his prodigal protégé (and thus wins Caelius's renewed loyalty ever after). Clodius's funder as recently as a month or so earlier, Crassus, joins in the defense.[45] Perhaps the wealthy financier (Caelius's other mentor) is concerned about the Egyptian dictator[46] repaying his debts. Whatever Crassus's motive, the two Claudians do not have the resources to outbid him for the Jurists' sympathies.

Nevertheless, Clodia and Clodius proceed with the prosecution of Caelius, much to Cicero's consternation. At trial, he addresses Clodia:

> *quoniam mente nescio qua effrenata atque praecipiti in forum deferri iudiciumque voluisti* (*Pro Caelio* 35 xrl.us/bi mb5j)

> [B]ecause of a mind I find incomprehensible, unbridled and headlong you choose to bring suit in the Roman Forum!

Contrary to assertions by some commentators that Cicero uses, in effect, "magical powers" (sardonically: Thomas Alan Dorey, p. 175) to cast a spell over the 75 (or more[47]) Jurists sitting in judgment, it is this reader's view that Caelius could be successfully defended by a blindfolded second-year law student with her writing-hand tied behind her back.

Then as now, the burden of proof is on the accusing party.[48] The prosecution's case for *Vis* boils down to Clodius's unsupported assertions and hearsay, which in turn are based upon his sister Clodia's uncorroborated allegations.

Had Clodius evidence more concrete to present, responding to it would not have been delegated to Crassus – who, whatever his merits as a military commander and financial operator, is not in Cicero's league as an orator. The first narrative a juror hears, even if presented as a hypothetical, is very hard to dislodge from that juror's mind.[49] Clodius – whose oratorical skills are formidable (Tatum, p. 41), Cicero's snarky remarks notwithstanding – would not delegate the prosecution's main case to a substitute orator. Likewise, were Clodius's presentation at all convincing, it would necessitate Cicero responding to it himself.

Thus, it is more likely than not that the only available witness to anything resembling the poisoning of Dio is Clodia, who claims Caelius has similarly tried to poison her. If the jury were to believe Caelius has attempted to poison Clodia to cover up her alleged discovery of his involvement with the poisoning of Dio, *ipso facto*, they might well believe that Caelius is guilty of the predicate crime as well.

Hence, the contest boils down to 'he said/she said' – with the burden of proof resting upon 'she', and therefore Clodia's credibility *must be* called into question by the defense.

Both Clodia and Caelius are sufficiently prominent that the Jurists are already well acquainted with their respective reputations (the original meaning of a "jury of peers"). Cicero, his numerous *non sequiturs* notwithstanding, all but concedes what everyone already knows: Caelius is a garden-variety Roman playboy. However, as they also know, Clodia is a one-woman *Satyricon*. How could there not be at least a *reasonable doubt* as to her account of what actually has happened?

The coinage of patriarchal attitude has two sides: patronization and paternalism. Masculine self-image is not well disposed to watching another man bullying an innocent woman. Clodia is the widow of an honorable and honored Consul of the Roman Empire. There must have been social intercourse, at one time or another, between Senators sitting on the Jury and Celer and his wife – as well as Caelius. It is inconceivable that any experienced trial attorney (and none has more jury-savvy than Cicero) would claim that such widow has engaged in the *public* conduct Cicero describes – unless he were completely confident that the Jurists already believe it to be so.[50] Thus, a relaxed Cicero feels free to pepper his oration with characteristically saucy sarcasm.[51]

This is where the matter inevitably becomes speculative, but it is also the point of intersection with *Carmen* 67: Clodia is no fool by anyone's account. She must know what will be the tenor of Cicero's oration, because he long has been saying complementarily scandalous things about her brother Clodius.[52]

So, *why* does Clodia "unbridled and headlong … choose to bring suit"? Skinner (2010, p. 111) asks rhetorically: "Wasn't

Clodia's respectability already too compromised to be an effective witness?" Skinner's answer, in brief, is that Clodia's male relatives put her into this position, for their own ends.

But, in the same passage, Skinner quotes Cicero mocking one of Clodia's claims – that she has, with the consent of her relatives, manumitted the family slaves who might otherwise be called by the prosecution as supporting witnesses – as being the only time she has *ever* done *anything* consistent with the wishes of her male relatives.[53]

In my view, Clodia does not expose herself to this degree of public contumely for anyone's purposes other than her own.

Here the plot thickens. It is noteworthy that Austin and a number of subsequent commentators have taken the view that Caelius must have done *something* related to the violence against the Egyptian emissaries. But, how can the critics be so sure? Because of claims made by Clodia's *brother* (or a family retainer using his name)?

Yet, Austin (p. 153) states categorically: "[T]here must have been some truth at the bottom of such persistent rumours." Dorey (p. 177) agrees:

> [T]here can be little doubt that Caelius had taken some part in the campaign of persecution and intimidation directed against the Alexandrian envoys. Otherwise the charge *de Alexandrinorum pulsatione Puteolana* [<of the assault on the Egyptians at Pozzuoli>] would have been inexplicable.

Austin and Dorey here seem to imply that an innocent man would not be prosecuted for a crime, even by those with a personal stake in a guilty verdict.

Wiseman (1987, p. 66) suggests mere motive and opportunity all but necessitate guilt:

> For a young man of such ability and such ambition, the murderous power game of Ptolemy's threatened kingdom must have been irresistibly attractive.

Tatum (p. 209), more cautiously, notes that Caelius's guilt "in view of his unscrupulous ambitions, lies well within the boundaries of possibility." Hejduk, judiciously, does not address the issue of Caelius's guilt or innocence.

Skinner (2010, p. 98), though she does not explicitly commit herself, observes:

> [M]any commentators suspect that Caelius, for all his bonhomie, was quite possibly implicated in some of the criminal acts alleged, specifically those involving aggression against foreign ambassadors.
>
> ..... Personal attacks on prosecutors and their witnesses, unimpeded by the rules of the court, were an integral part of the defense tool kit .... even though such transgressions might have seemed beside the point.

Then as now, whether testifying for the prosecutor/plaintiff or the defense, in matters both criminal and civil, the credibility of any witness who testifies may be impugned by opposing counsel. If the witness can be shown to have flaunted one set of social norms, it is perfectly permissible, then as now, for a jury to infer that the witness may likewise be flaunting the social norm that prohibits giving false testimony. Of course, virtually no modern court would allow an attorney to go to the lengths in attacking a witness's credibility as Cicero does in *Pro Caelio*. But, it would be poor trial practice for an attorney not to push the envelope, in this respect, as far as the court would allow.

Notably, of the 80 sections into which scholars have divided *Pro Caelio*, by my count 29 of them[54] are devoted to Cicero's defending against the prosecution's attacks on *Caelius's* sexual conduct. Unlike Cicero's attacks on Clodia's character, it cannot credibly be argued that such a lengthy defense by Cicero of Caelius's sex life is mere comic relief inserted to amuse and distract a jury in a holiday mood. The only explanation for the length and depth of this portion of his oration is that Cicero is aware that the prosecution's charges of sexual impropriety are potentially as damaging to Caelius's credibility as are Cicero's in relation to Clodia.

As noted, neither young Atratinus, speaking first for the prosecution, nor old Balbus, speaking last, directly take on the charges relating to *Vis*. Unfortunately, transcripts of their orations no longer exist – if ever they did. But, the inference to be drawn from Cicero's oration is that general charges of sexual impropriety and loose living, and Caelius's involvement with Clodia in particular, are not merely the thrust of two of the three prosecution orations – they are more or less the entirety.

His own client's sexual mores and general character having been attacked at length is further reason that Cicero *must* respond in kind regarding Clodia's reputation.

Skinner (2010, p. 109, citing David W Madsen) continues:

> For all its dexterity, however, Cicero's defense has been judged inadequate, since it dwells largely on the absurdities of the bathhouse caper and fails to come to grips with the underlying question of Caelius's dealings, if any, with [Ptolemy] Auletes. That lack of substance, in turn, has prompted deep doubts about the defendant's innocence of wrongdoing, particularly in harassing the Alexandrian embassy, another item in the indictment, and even the murder of Dio (*Cael.* 23).

Pace Madsen, I have read not a few lengthy treatments of a number of controversial, high-profile trials. I cannot recall another (with the exception of the Oscar Wilde debacle[55]) in which defense counsel succeeds as spectacularly as does Cicero in his representation of Caelius. Not only is Caelius acquitted; the prosecution, in particular Clodia, is *routed*.

Even the ostensible motive for bringing the trial – to prevent another prosecution of Atratinus's father, Bestia (*Pro Caelio* 56) – ultimately fails.[56]

By contrast with the 29 sections in which Cicero defends Caelius against charges of sexual immorality, Cicero disposes of the charges of *Vis* in a mere two (23 and 24) because the "lack of substance" is in the charges themselves, not in Cicero's handling of the case. Hence, unlike the charges of immoral living and, more to the point for our purposes, the charge that Caelius has attempted to poison Clodia, Cicero is confident that Crassus has already disposed of Clodius's accusations of *Vis* to the Jurists' satisfaction.

As noted above, the burden of proof rests with the party bringing an action at law. It is perfectly permissible in modern trial practice for the defense to rest its case as soon as the plaintiff or the prosecution rests its own case. The defense need "come to grips" with nothing at all. It need not dispel "deep doubts" about the defendant's innocence; in a criminal matter, it is the prosecutor who must dispel *any* doubts as to *guilt*.

Citing Erich Gruen (pp. 306-7 xrl.us/bmegct) and Wiseman (1985 [*or* 1987], p. 67), Skinner proceeds:

> One influential theory holds that Caelius was assisting Auletes on behalf of Pompey, who sought to benefit politically by restoring the king, his friend, and that this transfer of allegiance prompted Clodius to retaliate by supporting Atratinus's case.

In the cited pages, Gruen does indicate that Pompey stands to gain by the restoration of Ptolemy Auletes to the Egyptian throne, that while in Italy Ptolemy stays at one of Pompey's estates, that Pompey is already rumored to have been behind the political violence on behalf of Ptolemy, and thus a strike at Caelius for involvement with Ptolemy is a strike at Pompey himself. From this Gruen surmises: "[T]he adherents of Clodius were equally anxious to destroy Pompey's standing. They lurked behind the accusation of Caelius."

Wiseman presents his theory thus (1987, p. 67):

> Caelius' activities in the period from September 57 [BCE] to March 56 are best understood on the following hypothesis: that he was working secretly for Ptolemy (therefore, in effect, in Pompey's interests), and that when this became known to Clodius and his sister it caused a sudden breaking-off of relations at both the personal and political level.

These arguments are circular: Caelius is guilty of *Vis* because the two Clodians are prosecuting him to harm Pompey; therefore, Caelius is guilty of aiding Pompey by committing *Vis*.

Tatum, as noted, allows that Caelius's involvement in the political violence charged is *possible*, because of the opportunity for financial and political gain, Caelius's taste for high living, and his family's business interests in Africa. But as to viewing Pompey as the behind-the-scenes target of the prosecution of Caelius, Tatum (pp. 209-10) writes (with accompanying citations to the above-cited passages in Gruen and Wiseman):

> Whether Caelius had by late 57 allied himself to Pompey and whether that caused the rupture with Clodia and her brother must be deemed extremely uncertain ..... The trial has been interpreted as another of the strikes against Pompey's assumption of the assignment to restore the king [Ptolemy Auletes]. However, inasmuch as Pompey had removed himself from the competition after the senate's censure in February, this hypothesis must be rejected. Indeed, Pompey's presence goes remarkably undetectable in the testimonia to Caelius' trial. It seems more likely that Caelius was nobody's proxy: his own enemies sought to ruin him.

In other words, whatever may be the calculations of young Atratinus and old Balbus, Clodia's and Clodius's motives for the prosecution of Caelius are *personal*, not *business*. Hence, Cicero's focus on Clodia's character and motives is precisely on point: It is her brother Clodius's charges of *Vis* that are the 'sideshow'. Cicero, refusing to be distracted as a novice might, instead zeroes in on the real *casus belli:* Clodia's personal enmity toward Caelius. In turn, *Carmen* 67 relates the slave-girl gossip regarding the circumstances under which this enmity has arisen.

Of course, I am not disinclined to believe that where there is smoke, there is likely to be fire. But, to the extent that Caelius is impliedly to some degree guilty of *Vis* because a *whiff* of Pompeian smoke may be wafting from off-stage into the Roman Forum that day, *a fortiori*, the *clouds* of smoke with Clodia as their source strongly imply she is the Mt. Vesuvius behind the prosecution.

Cicero's *Pro Caelio*, in certain sections, may fairly be judged misogynistic, classist, ageist, patronizing, flippant, bombastic, bathetic, egotistical, and just plain *mean*. But, Cicero's defense of Caelius is far from *inadequate*.

In sum, whatever Caelius may actually be guilty of regarding *Vis*, the extant record, from a jurisprudential standpoint, would not warrant a contemporary cop on the beat to conduct a stop-and-frisk.

Instead, the evidence, such as it is, points to Caelius's having attempted to poison Clodia, because the alleged victim of such an attempt is there in court to so testify.

Regarding the charge of poisoning, a brief comment by Austin (p. 153) parallels his remark as to Caelius's putative guilt for *Vis:* "[H]ere again the story of the prosecution is so circumstantial that there must have been some underlying stratum of truth." With the exception of this conclusory assertion, none of the commentators cited herein, nor any other I have been able to uncover, has addressed the simple question: *Has* Caelius attempted to poison Clodia?

If he has not, I see no plausible reason why Clodia would publicly expose herself as she does here. But, if indeed Caelius has attempted to do so, then I think it quite plausible that a strong-willed woman not to be trifled with, such as Clodia, is demanding her day in court to put her case against Caelius before a jury of their peers.

Assuming Caelius is innocent of the charge of *Vis* (the surviving record, including that of subsequent ancient historians, provides no reason to believe he is guilty), and thus there is nothing of that nature that Caelius feared Clodia would expose, *why* then would Caelius attempt to poison Clodia? The precise details can never be known. But, Clodia's slavegirls apparently have made *their* views known to others – as Catullus reveals in *Carmen* 67.

Whatever actually has happened, by claiming that she has discovered a plot by Caelius to poison Dio, Clodia ensures that the trial will be momentous, as befits a *Diva* <Goddess>.[57] A failed attempt to poison her that grew out of a mere romantic rupture is not a capital offense; *Vis* is.

If these rumored surrounding circumstances are true – *ie*, a *mendaci ventre* <lying belly/womb> (67:48) that apparently has not led to the marriage of Clodia and Caelius – Clodia might claim, out of mere spite, that Caelius has attempted to poison her. However, if he *has* in fact tried to poison her, nonetheless the circumstances set forth in *Carmen* 67 are not such as would likely win a jury's sympathy. For that reason Clodia would still not want to raise them in her testimony.

Further, making public these circumstances would not reflect well on *Caelius* either – a reason Cicero would not want to pursue that line of inquiry beyond mere assertion of a romantic rupture and subsequent enmity – as Cicero repeats *seven* times, without specifying what those circumstances were.[58]

It is likely that Cicero himself does not know what really has transpired between Clodia and Caelius, because criminal defense attorneys often *do not want to know* if their client is guilty, lest 'guilty knowledge' of their own compromise their integrity before the court.

Yet, it may be that Cicero is worried that Clodia's accusation against Caelius is *substantially* true. The rumors Catullus publishes in the final verse of *Carmen* 67 about what really has happened between Clodia and Caelius have probably begun circulating before the trial. In which case, the Jurists too have heard them. Cicero can afford to give short shrift to the charge of political violence because, as far is known from surviving documents, there are no witnesses and no other evidence to connect Caelius to those crimes. Whereas, the alleged victim herself has testified regarding the charge of attempting to poison her – adding corroborating testimony to the onus of motive and opportunity. If all the details of the breakup are put into the record, the Jurists may be more inclined to believe Clodius tried to poison Clodia – irrespective of the charges of *Vis*.

Precisely because he fears it is substantially true, Cicero goes to some length in his oration to cast as preposterous Clodia's version of the who-what-where-and-when of Caelius's alleged plot to poison her (*Pro Caelio* 66 xrl.us/bkpfq4). But, Clodia's account does not strike this reader as out-of-line with the soundness of conception, and competence of execution (or lack thereof), of crime plots often uncovered in the news of today.

The Play's the Thing

Mid-oration, almost as if auditioning for one of Clodia's plays, Cicero engages in the role-playing of several characters (*ie*, *prosopopoeia*, a rhetorical device of Greek origin, perfected by Cicero). One such character is her brother Clodius, who, as the second prosecution orator, must have been livid – much to Cicero's and the spectators' mirth. In this role (the reader can almost hear the acerbic jocularity in his voice), Cicero taunts Clodia:

> *sumam aliquem ac potissimum minimum fratrem qui est in isto genere urbanissimus qui te amat plurimum qui propter nescio quam credo timiditatem et nocturnos quosdam inanis metus tecum semper pusio cum maiore sorore cubitabat eum putato tecum loqui quid tumultuaris soror quid insanis quid clamorem exorsa verbis parvam rem magnam facis vicinum adulescentulum aspexisti candor huius te et proceritas voltus oculique pepulerunt saepius videre voluisti fuisti non numquam in isdem hortis vis nobilis mulier illum filium familias patre parco ac tenaci habere tuis copiis devinctum non potes calcitrat respuit repellit non putat tua dona esse tanti confer te alio habes hortos ad tiberim ac diligenter eo loco paratos quo omnis iuventus natandi causa venit hinc licet condiciones cotidie legas cur huic qui te spernit molesta es (Pro Caelio 36 xrl.us/bigkhi)*

I will choose someone – your ablest and littlest brother – who is the most 'sophisticated' of his generation, who loves you the mostest, who (for I know not *how long*) as a little boy bedded beside big sister. (Why? A certain silly fear and anxiety about the dark, *I trust*.)

I think *he* would inquire of you:

"What *drama*, Sis! What *craziness!* What a commotion out of something that started with *a few little words!*

"You scoped the young neighbor: His dazzle and size, his face and eyes, had struck your fancy. You wanted to see him more often. You were not infrequently in the same pleasure-groves.

"A noblewoman, you want to make a house-slave of this son of a grasping, tightfisted father – by chaining him to your generosity. You aren't able – he kicks, he bucks, he rejects. He reckons your gifts to be not worth their price."

Cicero here seeks to remind the Jurists that (reputedly) Clodia's 'special relationship' with Clodius begins when her brother is quite young, and that this is consistent with Cicero's claim that *imbecillus* <poor defenseless> Caelius is not to be blamed for having been seduced by a libidinous older woman (a double standard based upon age, not gender).

Further, Cicero posits (through the 'voice' of Clodius) that the anger and attendant breakup that lead to her charges against Caelius arise merely from his romantic rejection of her. Yet, in doing so, Cicero subverts his own claim by having 'Clodius' mockingly point out that this is an almost trivial reason for bringing this *insanis* <craziness> into the Roman Forum in a trial for a capital offense.

As is clear from his personal correspondence, Cicero knows Clodia to be politically astute. Indeed, he himself has called upon her services in an attempt to smooth-over with Metellus Nepos, her husband's brother, relations that have been severely strained because of Cicero's extra-judicial executions of several of the Catilinarian conspirators (*Familiares* 5.2.6 xrl.us/bifmmi).

Moreover, moments before in his oration, Cicero role-plays Clodia's ancestor Appius Claudius ("the Blind") Caecus, asking Clodia angrily:

> *ideone ego pacem pyrrhi diremi ut tu amorum turpissimorum cotidie foedera ferires ideo aquam adduxi ut ea tu inceste uterere ideo viam munivi ut eam tu alienis viris comitata celebrares* (*Pro Caelio* 34 xrl.us/bimb5f)

For *this* did I derail a *peace pact* with Pyrrhus – so that *you* could forge the filthiest of *love pacts* daily? For *this* did I build the Appian Aqueduct – so that *you* could wash after *incest*? For *this* did I build the Via Appia – so that *you* could frequent it with a *throng* of men who're *not* your husband?

By having 'Caecus' denounce Clodia for promenading along the Via Appia attended by a group of (presumably young) male admirers, Cicero further undermines his own 'woman-scorned' explanation for her testimony against Caelius. There are too many 'fish' in the Tiber for her to subject herself to Cicero's withering denunciation merely because of one who got away.

Further, why would Caelius need to borrow gold from *Clodia* if to finance *Vis* on behalf of Ptolemy Auletes? The king has *already* donated the royal sum of 35 million denarii (Wiseman 1987, p. 58) to Caesar and Pompey for distribution to vacillating Senators. Why would Caelius *borrow* from Clodia – for a *hidden* purpose – when the king would *gladly* 'gift' the necessary funds, and then some, for the very same purpose?

Therefore, I do not think that Cicero believes romantic rejection is the *only* reason Clodia is accusing Caelius of attempting to poison her, and I do not believe Clodia cares enough about her family's political scheming to submit herself to so much public obloquy by offering testimony that Caelius attempted to poison her – *unless* it bears *some* resemblance to the truth of the matter. Instead, I believe the final lines of *Carmen* 67 provide the key to understanding why Clodia has broken off relations with Caelius, and has prosecuted him for attempted poisoning.

Thus, the historical context in which *Carmen* 67 is written.

The Underlying Meaning of *Carmen* 67

They said you was high-clast, *well that was just a* lie.
(Elvis Presley)

The worst *poet* ever! (Clodia Metelli)

Carmen 67 is a *ratatouille* of (contemporaneously) known fact, gossip long circulating in Brescia, the tittle-tattle of Clodia's slave-girls, and perhaps some of the 'pillow talk' Catullus himself has at some time heard from Clodia. It is written post *Pro Caelio*, and thus Clodia no longer has a public reputation to lose. (Yet Catullus, her bitterly abject love-slave to the end, still refrains from unambiguously identifying her.[59])

Catullus, like Cicero unsure himself of the specifics of this and other rumored incidents from Clodia's past, shows off his flair for the Callimachean[60] by inventively reworking the *paraclausithyron* motif,[61] putting a bundle of 'dirty laundry' in the 'mouth' of the lady-in-question's House Door, which is personified as a slave-girl.

By having a slave-girl portal tell these tales, not only does Catullus distance himself from the claims; he also allows himself a certain amount of ambiguity, and even self-contradiction.

This song-poem reveals in its "maddeningly confusing" way (as is often the gossip of ancillaries) that Clodia comes of age in Brescia, about 40 miles northwest of fair Verona (perhaps during the 88-84 BCE political exile of Clodia's father, Appius Claudius Pulcher, a span during which Clodia's age is about 10-14).

Of this period (in whatever locale) in the lives of Appius Claudius's children, Wiseman writes:[62]

> It was later said of the youngest boy, Publius [*ie*, Clodius], that he sold himself for the pleasure of 'wealthy playboys'. We must remember the slanderous norms of Roman political invective; but it is likely enough that all five of the siblings made themselves agreeable to guests who could be of future value to their careers.

Balbus <"Baldy" (implying virility)> is the (adopted) son of Clodia's paternal grandfather, Appius Claudius Pulcher (Consul 143 BCE), and the father of Clodia's *vir* <husband>, Celer – thus confirming Thomas W Hillard's hypothesis.[63]

Celer, according to the gossipy Door, suffers erectile dysfunction (a topic Catullus really warms-up to). Perhaps the rumored dysfunction is severe enough to completely prevent penetration.[64] In any case, Celer is unable *zonam solvere virgineam* <to untie a virgin's *not*>. Further, Celer is *sterile semine* <with sterile seed>, and thus cannot provide Clodia with a male heir.[65]

While still in Brescia, Clodia has affairs with two men: one named Cornelius; the other, Postumius. The former may be the dedicatee of (at least the first 60 of) Catullus's *carmina* (*see* Appendix E); the ability to identity the latter figure might garner 'bonus points' for listeners/readers who are among the *cognoscenti* of Clodia's amorous adventures.

Upon her marriage to Celer (Caecilius I), probably arranged during her childhood, the couple reside in Verona in the house of Celer's father, Baldy.

Because of Celer's inadequacy in the boudoir, and Clodia's need for a male heir (as well as her need for physical intimacy), she chooses to conjugate instead with Celer's father, Baldy (the Door's revelation of which evokes Catullus's sarcasm and mock shock).

While Baldy is alive, Clodia's charms are his alone. After he dies, Clodia's attentions are directed elsewhere – but with no resultant male heir. Hence, upon the death of Celer (59 BCE), the house is conveyed to a male relative of his (and likely hers as well), the new Caecilius (II) in Clodia's life.

Last, but far from least, the song-poem relates in its final line (67:48) if not the exact details, then at a minimum the gist of what brings about Clodia's breakup with Caelius, and leads to her accusation that he has attempted to poison her: Clodia informs Caelius she is pregnant with their child. Caelius may not be as sanguine as Catullus at the thought of marriage to Clodia.[65.1] Also, he may doubt that he is the father. Apparently, so do her slave-girls: in the Door's words *mendaci ventre*

<a belly of lies>. Perhaps, on the pretense of financing a spectacle to advance his political career, Caelius borrows gold from Clodia, but instead uses it to obtain an abortifacient. He surreptitiously administers it, and the result is a *falsum* <miscarried> *puerperium* <literally: boy-birth (the *last* word of *Carmen* 67)>. Thus does Caecilius II inherit Clodia's original marital home.

Carmina 69 and 77, as well, may allude to Clodia's poisoning allegation against Caelius (reciprocally, *Carmen* 67 strengthens the case for identifying Catullus's Lesbia as Clodia Metelli). John Noonan (pp. 160, 163-64), building upon a conjecture by Nathan Dane, makes this case quite densely (and cogently) for 69:7-8, accenting his argument by noting a similar observation by Fordyce about 77:5-6. In demonstrating the Clodia/Lesbia connection herself, Hejduk (p. 145, n. 181) succinctly summarizes:

> Noonan (1979) suggests that the threat to women posed by the "plague" of Rufus's body odor alludes to allegations that Caelius was a poisoner of women; poem 77:5-6, in which the same Rufus is both "plague" [*pestis*] and "poison" [*venenum*], supports such a reading. In addition, "beast" (Latin *bestia* 69:8) was the cognomen of Lucius Calpernius Bestia .... [L]ike Caelius, Bestia was accused of poisoning women .... The poison Bestia supposedly used, aconite, called both "lady killer" (thelyphonon) and "beast bane" (therophonon), was foul smelling and inserted vaginally – all associations appropriate to the context here.

Aconite can be used as a lethal poison (Chan, p. 279), but also as an abortifacient (Barceloux, p. 737), and even, in smaller dosage, as a recreational drug (Cilliers and Retief, p. 90, n. 3).

In my reading, then, Carmen *67 indicates that, according to the gossip of Clodia's slave-girls, Clodia prosecutes Caelius for attempting to poison her by virtue of his administering an abortifacient that causes the miscarriage of a fetus who if born alive would have been Clodia's male heir.*

Catullus's *Carmen* 67, in Translation

[Interlocutor]

Oh joy to a sweet husband, joy to a father – *salutations*
And, may goodness redound to you by God's grace,
Miss Door, whom they say to have slaved *benignly*
for *Baldy* earlier – when Senior *himself* held the seat of power,
yet whom (they rumor) have reneged on responsibility   5
ever since Senior was laid to rest, serving *malignly*
    the vow made in marriage.

Tell us *why* you would be rumored to have changed course
from having slaved so faithfully for the Old Master?

[Door]

No fault is *mine!* Although, it is *said* to be mine.
(I must now likewise please *Caecilius*, having been
    conveyed to *him*.)   10
Nor can anyone accuse me of any *wrong!*

To be sure, the *townspeople:* "The *Door* did it!"
When anything *whatsoever* is discovered to have not gone
    well,
they *all* shout at *me,* "It's *your* fault, Door!"

[Interlocutor]

Saying the word is not enough;   15
instead, make it so that anyone can *see* and *feel.*

[Door]

How *can* I? No one *asks* – or *wants* to find out.

[Interlocutor]

Indubitably, *we* do! Tell us!

[Door]

Well then … *first* of all: The 'virgin' brought us
    was a *fraudulent conveyance!*
(Not that the groom *could have* touched her beforehand,   20
he who, *little* dagger drooping limper than the letter *lambda,*
never got it up to half-mast!)

But, the *father* is said to have violated the son's *marriage
bed*, and to have defiled the disgraced domicile –
whether because *his* filthy mind was ablaze
    with blind lust   25
or because the impotent son was with sterile seed,
and *she* sought – from *whatever* source – that stronger
muscle that could untie a virgin's *not*.

[Interlocutor]

You tell a tale about an *excellent* parent of *admirable* piety –
who would *squirt* in his own son's *lap!*   30

[Door]

And not only is *he himself* said to have had this carnal
    knowledge.
Brescia, set 'neath China Hill look-out,
where the yellow Mello river gently flows;
Brescia, beloved mother of *Verona mia* –
even it tells tales of amours with
    Postumius and Cornelius,   35
with whom *both*, she committed the sin of *adultery!*

[Interlocutor]

At *this*, someone might say, "How did *you* learn these things,
    Miss Door,
who never has license to absent the Master's threshold,
nor hear *townspeople?* Instead, you've been affixed to the
lintel here; so your function is to admit (or to *not admit!*)
    to the home.   40

[Door]

I often heard *her* talking – in a *furtive* voice
with only slave-girls present – about her *outrageousness*,
naming the names we spoke about.
(She naturally would have been hoping me to be
    with neither tongue nor ear.)

She added *en passant* a certain someone whose name   45
I don't want to say, lest he *arch* russet eyebrows.
He's a tall man who at one time made *major arguments*
against a *belly of lies* over a *miscarried* boy-birth!

Coda

With the sole exception of Clodia (as far as is known), in the years to come all of the foregoing personages suffer a violent death or (in the case of Catullus) die otherwise prematurely.

- Catiline: Slain plunging into the heat of a battle he knows he is doomed to lose against superior force – his head sent back to Rome (62 BCE). Enraged, his plebeian supporters burn to the ground the Senate House.

- Crassus: After being slain in battle with Parthia (Afghanistan/Iran; 53 BCE), his head reportedly is used as a stage prop to entertain the Parthian King.

- Clodius: Killed by his rival Milo's private militia, or otherwise assassinated (52/53 BCE). Clodius's plebeian supporters, like Catiline's a decade earlier, burn down the Senate House.

- Pompey the Great: Assassinated while haplessly seeking military assistance in Egypt, his head presented to his rival for power Caesar (48 BCE).

- Caelius: Slain while rebelling against Caesar (48 BCE).

- Caesar: Literally stabbed in the back by Senate colleagues (44 BCE).

- Cleopatra and Mark Antony: Double suicides, 11 days apart, after decisive defeat by Octavian, the future Caesar Augustus (30 BCE).

- Cicero: On orders of Mark Antony, slain while in flight, his head and hands nailed to the rostrum in the Roman Forum (43 BCE).

Plutarch (49.5) tells this 'just-so story' by way of epitaph for Cicero:

> I learn that [Caesar Augustus, the first Roman Emperor – the type of eventuality Cicero gave his life opposing] a long time after this, paid a visit to one of his daughter's sons; and the boy, since he had in his hands a book of

Cicero's, was terrified and sought to hide it in his gown; but Caesar saw it, and took the book, and read a great part of it as he stood, and then gave it back to the youth, saying: "A learned man, my child, a learned man and a lover of his country."

In death, as in life, setting the standard for future love poets, Catullus is relieved of this mortal coil around age 30 (*c.* 54 BCE) – perhaps, as with Elvis, due to 'exhaustion'.

The circumstance of Clodia's death is lost to history. Clio's silence may suggest such circumstance was merely advanced age. She is last heard-of in a 44 BCE letter (*see* n. 44 below) written by Cicero (who seemingly is still reticent to meet her in-person) – a wealthy widow in middle age with an estate (coveted by Cicero) on the River Tiber, in which young men swim *au naturale.*

Part II: The Spinach and Broccoli

Cinna: *I am Cinna the* poet, *I am Cinna the* poet.
4th Citizen: *Tear him for his bad verses, tear him for his bad verses.* (William Shakespeare)

The difficulties, such as they are, have been for the most part created by modern scholars. (Peter Green)

[O]nce we have been sufficiently dirty-minded to understand Catullus' words, the poem will become so perspicuous that the reader will be left wondering why the fuss was made at all.
(Giuseppe Giangrande)

Why, after centuries of study and commentary by brilliant scholars, does *Carmen* 67 still remain a "maddeningly confusing" "riddle" and "enigma"? [66]

Among the preceding quotations, Shakespeare sardonically comments on blaming a poet for the difficulty in understanding his or her verses. Green (2005, p. 250) puts the blame "for the most part" on "modern scholars". Giangrande (p. 85), concurring with Green's general point, narrows the focus to insufficiency of prurience.

Copley (1949, p. 245) concurs, more bluntly:

> It sometimes happens that a work of classical antiquity has had its meaning obscured by the sheer bulk of the scholarly efforts that have been expended upon it. This has been the fate of Catullus' *ianua*-poem [<door-poem>].

Giangrande (p. 84) caustically cites a representative example:

> Whenever the critics complain about the "obscurities" that surround a poem, it is a good rule to ask oneself whether the poet is really to be blamed, or rather the critics themselves are at fault. An instructive case is represented by A.P. XII 129 (= Gow Page 760), where scholars first created *aus der Luft* [<out of air>] a character, then tried forcibly – and, not surprisingly, in vain – to insert it into the epigram, and then shed crocodile tears over the poem they had thus messed up, complaining that the poet was not clear. The inane struggles of the

critics with the ghost-character, whose identity nobody troubled to check up, lasted for no less than a couple of centuries, until it was shown that the troublemaker was a figment of the critics' fantasy.

Exactly the same has happened to Catullus 67: **instead of reading what the poet has to say, the critics first created one husband too many and then complained that the poem was obscure.** [Emphasis added.]

Green (2005, p. 250) highlights an example of another type of scholarly contribution to the overall puzzlement:

[Godwin] adds to the confusion by his claim that Quinn and Goold identify the father and son of [verses] 1-6 with those of 20-27, which they do not.

Thus, not only do scholars disagree as to what words Catullus actually has written (*facta* vs *pacta, etc*), and what he actually means by those words (*prior* = previous *or* previou*sly?*), but even about what other contemporary scholars themselves have written about *Carmen* 67.

As noted at the outset: Without the countless hours of painstaking academic scholarship over the course of the centuries, we would not have an intelligible text at all.

And yet, it need be asked in regard to the various readings of *Carmen* 67: Why, well more than four hundred years after humanist scholar Petrus Victorius has identified the Lesbia of Catullus's poetry as the Clodia Metelli of Cicero's prose (Austin, 149-50) – notwithstanding much speculation about who did what, where did they do it, and particularly about the identity of the tall russet-haired paramour of the final verses – no commentator I have encountered has yet addressed the issue: Who was the *woman?* (But, *see* n. 3 below.)

Why has no one yet entertained in print (in the world of Anglophone scholarship, at least) even a hypothesis that the willful woman of *Carmen* 67 who is associated, however indirectly, with a man of the same clan name, "Caecilius", as Clodia's husband, and who has had a love affair with a tall russet-browed man (*eg*, Marcus Caelius {"Rusty"} Rufus) who, in turn, has been involved in a major lawsuit (*eg, Pro Caelio*), is *lesbia nostra* <*Our* Lesbia>?[67]

By anyone's count, more than two dozen of Catullus's song-poems are about Clodia (in my reading, closer to three dozen). About which woman, other than Clodia, would Catullus go to the trouble of composing a minor masterpiece that delves into so much detail about her past, and that requires at least two readers for its public performance? Of which man, other than Clodia's husband, Celer, would Catullus take such 'cherished delight' in describing so graphically that man's inability to satisfy his wife's *ardour?*

Which tall russet-browed man is the defendant in what still stands as the ancient world's third most famous trial? (The only two better known are the trial of the Hebrew prophet Jesus, and that of the Athenian philosopher Socrates.)

Surprisingly, Green (2005, p. 250) essentially dismisses such questions as nonessential: "Neither the wife, nor her earlier husband and father-in-law, nor the **rufous** stranger are named, or really need to be." [Emphasis added.]

I am puzzled that a scholar as careful and cautious as Green would make such an unqualified statement *a priori* (but, *see* p. 81 below). On the previous page he himself (in accord with Copley and Wiseman) observes:

> Catullus was clearly dealing with a scandal well known to the members of his Verona circle, but which remains obscure to us. **Yet he hoped to be read by a wider audience and to survive for posterity**, so unless this was a purely private lampoon, included by some editor in error after Catullus's death, we have to assume that half the fun for the poet was leaving a row of tantalizing clues for reader or listener to piece together. [Emphasis added.]

In other words, if posterity is unable to "piece together" the "tantalizing clues", then Catullus has failed to accomplish one of his major goals for this song-poem; in Giangrande's terms: The poet is at fault. Apparently aware of this pitfall, Green provides the potential escape hatch of "a purely private lampoon, included by some editor in error after Catullus's death." *(Editora, culpa tua est!)*[68]

First Principle: Yes, Virginia, There Is a Lesbia –
and Her Historical Name is Clodia Metelli

My reading of *Carmen* 67 accepts Victorius's identification (and that of most commentators in the centuries since) of Cicero's Clodia Metelli as Catullus's Lesbia. Absent a 'long-form birth certificate' for Lesbia (or a fortuitous archeological discovery), this identification cannot be made with *absolute certainty*. However, as Green (2005, p. 4) tellingly notes:

> The cumulative evidence for this identification is in fact a good deal solider than that for many other firmly held beliefs about the ancient world.

Nevertheless, Lesbia's real-life identity (or even her *existence*, as shall be seen) remains a matter of scholarly dispute. For this reason, a review of the relevant evidence follows:

In the second half of the 1st Century CE, the family of a wealthy widow whose troth had been sought by Apuleius[69] brings suit against him for allegedly using witchcraft to induce the widow to marry him. They cite as evidence of witchery his use of pseudonyms instead of the real names of those he has written about. In his defense, Apuleius reasons thus:

> *igitur opera accusent c catullum quod lesbiam pro clodia nominarit*

> Therefore, they would indict *Gaius Catullus* because he would use the name "Lesbia" for Clodia! (*Apologia* 1:10 xrl.us/bmdsvr)

... without telling us this adulterous Clodia's married name (apparently presuming that readers would already *know*).

Hence, whatever her married name, the actual first name of Lesbia is "Clodia".

Catullus begins *Carmen* 79: *lesbius est pulcher* <Lesbius is pretty> xrl.us/bmfbvz, strongly implying that Lesbi*us* is brother to Lesbi*a*, and that he has the masculine form ("Pulcher") of the same *cognomen* <nickname> as she ("Pulchra"), *ie*, Publius Clodius Pulcher/Clodia Metelli Pulchra.

And so, Catullus teasingly indicates that the Clodia in question is a sister of Clodius.

Though Clodius has two sisters in addition to Clodia Metelli, one is already widowed and the other long divorced before an adulterous affair with Catullus is likely to have commenced (Green 2005, p. 294).

Further, I find no credible evidence that either of these two sisters change her clan name from "Claudia" to "Clodia"; nor any evidence at all that either has reason to do so for the purpose of promoting Clodius's political career; nor warrant to believe that either of his brothers change their clan name to "Clodius". (*See* Appendix D.)

Hejduk (pp. 6-8) observes that in *Carmen* 58 xrl.us/bmfbrv, a "Caelius" is informed that *Lesbia Nostra* is on street corners and in back alleys of Rome playing the role of a streetwalker – with a supporting cast of young aristos; in *Carmen* 69 xrl.us/bmfbv9, a "Rufus" is accused of having underarms that smell like a goat; in *Carmen* 77 xrl.us/bmfbxz, a "Rufus" is accused by Catullus of betraying their friendship and destroying Catullus's happiness; and in *Carmen* 100, a "Caelius" is wished success (in my reading, sarcastically) in a same-sex infatuation xrl.us/bmfbyy. Hejduk points out that even if the referents were four *different* people (unlikely), if any *one* were Marcus Caelius Rufus, Lesbia is all but certainly identified as the Clodia Metelli of Cicero's *Pro Caelio*.

Perhaps, in the *lepidus* phrasing of Green (2005, p. xi), Wiseman (1969, p. 56) is being "elegantly combative" in interpreting the same evidence thus:

> The identification of Caelius Rufus as the Rufus of poems 69 and 77 and/or the Caelius of poems 58 and 100 is another apparent argument for the identity of this Clodia and Lesbia which collapses at close inspection. Catullus' Caelius was Veronese; M. Caelius Rufus came from Interamnia Praetuttiorum [ancient Teramo]. Catullus' Caelius was a trusted friend and confidant of the poet in his affair with Lesbia; Catullus' Rufus was a treacherous rival, one of Lesbia's lovers.

That Clodia Metelli's Caelius is from Teramo is no more a bar to his having been at some point in his youth Veronese, than is Cicero's roots in Arpino or Catullus's own Veronese past a bar to their both being Roman. (*See* also p. 83 below.)

That a trusted friend and confidant can become also a treacherous rival in love is a staple of Blues and country music, among other narrative forms.[70]

Catullus prays that his poetry will *plus uno maneat perenne saeclo* <remain a perennial more than a *century*> (*Carmen* 1:10 xrl.us/bmfbzg). Does Catullus *not* realize that future readers will associate the names "Caelius" and "Rufus" with *Caelius Rufus?* If Catullus intends otherwise, would he not use another name for the subject(s) of *Carmina* 58, 69, 77, and 100? – *eg, rufulum* <Little Rufie> in *Carmen* 59.

For those who trust poetic sense more than lawyerly argument, or are more comfortable when there is agreement between the two, there is this observation by Quinn (1972b, p. 135): "[T]he Clodia painted by Cicero in his speech in defense of Caelius is Lesbia to the life."

It's Only Make Believe?[71]

It has been argued that even if Clodia Metelli is the model for Catullus's Lesbia, there has not been an actual romantic relationship between the two – Catullus is merely indulging in artistic fantasy. In fact, Clodia has barely noticed the young poet's existence, beyond perhaps requesting at a dinner gathering: "Please pass the canolis, Catullus."

A number of years ago, it was fashionable to posit that the entertainer Marilyn Monroe[72] was not caricaturing a certain sort of *woman*, but rather portraying a female *impersonator*. A friend of mine at the time was so adamant on this point that I did not dare inquire of her: *Whom*, then, are female impersonators *impersonating?*

In a vein somewhat akin, Niklas Holzberg takes the radically revisionist position that Lesbia does not *exist*,[73] except as Catullus's contribution to the literary stereotype of the *hetaera* <cultured courtesan – typically a freed Greek slave>.

In addition, the individual most readers think is Clodia's husband, Celer, is merely an (impliedly) imaginary client of this imaginary *hetaera*.[74] Further, Lesbius (79:1) is not Clodia/Lesbia's brother Clodius, but instead an (imagined) lover who shares her imagined enjoyment of fellatio.

Holzberg points out that, centuries after her death, (male) writers come to view Sappho herself as a *hetaera*. Thus, he argues, Catullus's choice of the name "Lesbia" is not an allusion to Sappho as a poetic Muse, but rather to Sappho's reputation (though false) as a *hetaera*.

Catullus is not the one, however, who imagines that Clodia Metelli and Marcus Caelius Rufus have had an affair. Instead (citing Wilfred Stroh), *Cicero* conjures up this affair (and apparently, a majority of Jurists – most, if not all, of whom *already know* Clodia and Caelius personally – believe in this imaginary affair that Cicero has conjured).[75]

Holzberg begins his article (p. 28):

> Our understanding of ancient erotic poetry has, in my opinion, been greatly furthered in recent years by the shift from an approach which sees the poetic world of Roman love elegy as the creation of mimesis to one which reads it as semiosis. The elegiac poet portrays neither experienced reality nor conditions at least conceivable as such, but constructs a fictional situation using certain literary motifs provided by generic tradition, and thus challenges the reader to a game of semiotics. The latter, conversant with the 'sign language' of the motifs – for example of *servitium amoris* [<love slave>] – will appreciate the poet's playful variations on a familiar theme and decipher the new meaning it has been given. Particularly significant here is, I find, the new perception of the two central characters in the elegiac world: the first-person *poeta/amator* [<poet/lover>] and his *puella* [<Mistress>] are both part of this fiction. The poet assumes the mask of an elegiac lover, playing the part as an actor would; he does not, then, re-enact his own experiences for an audience. In addition to this he designs the figure of the *puella*, who appears less as a character with its [*sic*] own personal profile and more as a typified representation, contrived in the main to reflect the poetic *ego*'s [<poetic persona's>] thoughts. Women such as Cynthia, Delia, and Corinna are, to use Alison Sharrock's very apt defi-

nition, the product of 'womanufacture', and their names therefore cannot be read as pseudonyms for real-life women.

In other words, one of the most transparently autobiographical poets in the history of verse is not holding a mirror up to himself and his world, but instead holding up a mirror (albeit with its own interesting curvature) to *prior verse* about the *hetaera* as literary stereotype.

And, for good measure (p. 29):

> The parallels drawn are not between poetry and reality, but between poetry and another form of fiction, since the Clodia in Cicero's *Pro Caelio* is certainly [*sic*] as much a product of 'womanufacture' as Catullus's Clodia.

It should be noted that in the same sentence that Apuleius names Clodia as Catullus's "Lesbia", he also names Hostia as Propertius's "Cynthia", and Plania as Tibullus's "Delia" (along with Metella, Clodia Metelli's daughter, as Ticidas's "Perilla").

Apuleius is silent about "Corinna", the name Ovid gives *his* faithless *inamorata*. But, Green (1982, p. 23), who (like Hejduk) does not allow literary theory to trump literary sense, makes this interesting observation:

> ... [W]hen we have made all possible allowance for literary borrowings and inventive fantasy, it seems an almost irresistible conclusion that Corinna was based, at least in part, on Ovid's mysterious first wife.

Holzberg does not provide examples of another such literary exercise in which the song-poet viciously attacks a number of personal acquaintances for being among the imaginary *hetaera's* imaginary clientele. (But, perhaps Catullus is writing of imaginary personal acquaintances.)

Realizing that Apuleius's defending himself against charges of witchcraft – because of his use of pseudonyms for *real* people – by referring to Catullus (as well others) as a precedent innocent of witchery, would make no sense if there were no real-life Clodia behind the pseudonym "Lesbia", Holzberg concedes (p. 29):

Obviously we cannot entirely rule out the possibility that there was a woman who in some measure inspired Catullus in his creation of Lesbia, and what Apuleius tells us (*Apol.* 10), i.e. that the name was a pseudonym for one Clodia, may have been the case.

Indeed. Nor can we *entirely* rule out the possibility that this woman – named "Clodia" who "in some measure" inspires Catullus in his creation of Lesbia (or, for that matter, Cicero's *Pro Caelio*) – is *not* the real-life Clodia Metelli. But, whatever may be inconclusive about this or that isolated datum of evidence, when the evidence is viewed in its totality, the skeptically minded cannot but wonder at such a 'massive coincidence' of recorded data pointing in the direction of *Our* Clodia.

Neither does Holzberg explain, more tellingly yet, why in *Carmen* 57 xrl.us/bmrbhg Catullus would use the real names of the great Caesar and of Mamurra, Caesar's chief engineer in the conquest of Gaul, in (repeatedly and explicitly) mocking both of them (accurately or inaccurately) for orally and anally accommodating other men's lust? Holzberg (p. 30) suggests the real-life Clodia may be someone of no more status than a freed slave once the property of the Claudian clan. Why then would Catullus go to such lengths to *hide* the real name of a mere freed slave who vaguely reminds Catullus of his 'imaginary' Lesbia, yet savage two of the most powerful personages of the day, Caesar and Mamurra – using their *real* names?[76]

The Day the Music Died

There are countless examples of pop tunes of the past century that are merely variations on well worn themes – the 'moon in June' sort of thing – in which the singer croons his or her love in the 1st person, without intending autobiographical significance. However, there are numerous exceptions, particularly in songs in which the beloved is *named*.

In the early hours of February 3, 1959, a single-engine plane crashes into a cornfield near Clear Lake, Iowa. All on board – the pilot, Roger Peterson, and his three passengers, known by their stage names "Big Bopper" Richardson, Ritchie Valens, and Buddy Holly – die on impact.[77]

Richardson's one pop hit, "Chantilly Lace", is merely a generic celebration of the hormones of youth. But, Ritchie Valens's "Donna" is about his feelings for the real-life Donna Ludwig. Holly's song "Peggy Sue" expresses how drummer Jerry Allison, its coauthor, feels about his recent breakup with the real-life Peggy Sue Gerron – whom Allison would eventually marry bit.ly/vIdo.

Paul Anka is still very much alive, and a highly compensated Las Vegas entertainer. His breakthrough hit, "Diana", remains his fans' favorite. It expresses Anka's boyish love for the real-life Diana Ayoub.[78] In "Oh! Carol", Neil Sedaka pines for Carole King.

Of course, these pop tunes offer-up emotions that, though sincere, are merely sentimental confections. By contrast, even the most juvenile of Catullus's paeans to Lesbia, *Carmen* 5, touches upon a profound theme: the brevity of life and the permanence of death:

> *soles occidere et redire possunt*
> *nobis cum semel occidit brevis lux*
> *nox est perpetua una dormienda* (4-6)

> The sun can set and rise;
> *our* brief light sets but once;
> *our* night's an endless sleep.

Had any of these four pop entertainers written not just one, but more than two dozen songs of Catullus's sensitivity about his feelings for the same woman, would anyone believe he were not singing about a real-life woman, rather than merely doing innovative variations on standard themes from the Great American Songbook?

To be sure, no trained artist creates works *in vacuo*. Opera sopranos often ask themselves, "How would Callas sing this aria?" bit.ly/vAds4X. Actors often ask themselves, "How would Brando or Leigh play this scene?" bit.ly/shHQnY.

Echos from other artists appear in virtually every artistic creation (though some 'echos' are more attenuated than others, as shall be seen, pp. 105-7). But, that's a different proposition than the assertion that an artist who presents a *body of work* as having been written from life nonetheless is *only* reworking fictive elements from other artists.

Anka's most famous composition, "My Way", was written specifically for Frank Sinatra. Yet, its theme of an aging Everyman proclaiming his uniqueness, as the end approaches, has made "My Way" perhaps the song most 'covered' by other artists. One artist that Anka explicitly cautioned *not* to perform this tune, because Anka considered it not suitable for him, is Elvis.[79] However, in this performance by Elvis two months before his death, it is hard to not feel that there is *something* of the autobiographical in it bit.ly/9V4x92.

E Pluribus Unum

Before proceeding, I should disclose that my own conceptual bias is universalist. In the literal sense, there was a decade of my early adulthood during which I was a member of the Unitarian/Universalist Association. As such, I visited a number of services at other houses of worship, across the denominational spectra of both Christianity and Judaism.

One Sunday I attended a service at a high Episcopal congregation, as well as the gathering for coffee or tea that followed. There I met the priest who had conducted the service. Upon identifying my own congregational affiliation of the time, he exclaimed, "Ohhh ... you must find this very *different!*" Not wanting to contradict my host upon first meeting him, I did not reveal that, on the contrary, I found it quite similar.

A group of people assemble one day per week in a quiet place set aside for that purpose. Someone learned in the traditions of that group presides. The congregation is welcomed, there is prayer, singing, a reading or two from a venerated text, a homily that in most cases is in some way grounded in the Golden Rule, followed by announcements, more singing, more prayer, and then refreshment afterward.

Of course, there are differences in details. I would not have visited so many different congregations had I not found the differences in details fascinating. But, I did not find them vital in their relation to ultimate questions, spiritual contemplation, or (hoped for) spiritual uplift.

... As Time Goes By

By way of a geopolitical analogy, the modern nation state is only a few centuries in existence. And, the contemporary "national-security state" did not emerge until the outbreak of European hostilities in August 1914.

But though in Italy some place names have changed, some places themselves have disappeared, others have come into existence relatively recently, and borders, particularly in the North, have shifted hither and thither over the centuries (mainly thither), nevertheless, Clodia, Catullus, Cicero, Caelius, and their ancient Roman circle consider themselves every bit as *Italian* as does former Prime Minister Silvio Berlusconi.

Though language is as socially constructed as a human behavior can be, and the existence of language is at most a few tens of thousands of years in duration, the language of educated Italians has been remarkably stable since the time of Cicero, Caesar, and Catullus. It might be said, without excessive exaggeration, that modern Italian is merely one dialect of ancient Latin (university-level English being another).

(A further personal disclosure is that I am not aware of anyone who exceeds my empathy for consenting adults pursuing their personal bliss in whatever safe and sane manner they prefer – on whatever terms they choose.)

The Fundamental Things Apply ...

Consistent with my universalist bias, I am highly skeptical that modern Italians (and the rest of the West), unlike the examples of their very similar language and sense of nationhood to that of two thousand years previous, conceptualize human sexuality, rooted as it is in hundreds of millions of years of biological evolution, in ways radically different from their ancient Roman antecedents.

To the contrary, I find even *less* difference between ancient Roman attitudes about sexuality – as revealed by the extant documents – and today's attitudes (or "ideology") than between ancient Latin and the language of modern Italians, or between ancient *Italia* and modern *Italia*.

What I do find, affirmatively, is that the attitudes of cultural conservatives such as Cicero, of cultural liberals such as Clodia/Lesbia, and of those such as Catullus torn from within by the conflicting imperatives of both, are barely distinguishable from those of today, but for two vital exceptions: Contemporary cultural liberals, unlike their ancient counterparts, have universalized human rights, irrespective of gender, class, ethnicity, and sexual preference; and, modern liberals and conservatives alike stand together against the exploitation of children.

The views expressed by Holzberg regarding the ways in which ancient Romans conceived of sexuality are shared, to one degree or another, by a number of other learned individuals, in and out of the academy. A passage from his article is being singled-out for detailed comment because he has condensed into less than a page ideas espoused by many other commentators and because underlying this position is the fallacy that in the words of Wiseman's chapter heading quoted above, ancient Rome is "a world not ours".

Pace Wiseman and Holzberg, ancient Rome is a world virtually identical to ours, save for details of no *essential* consequence to the understanding of *Catullus*. What distinguishes ancient Rome from today's world, as pertains to Catullan studies, is that because then as now power tends to corrupt and absolute power tends to corrupt absolutely, powerful ancient Romans engaged in extremes of sex, violence, and exploitation that shock contemporary sensibilities. But, these differences are *quantitative*, not *qualitative*.

Catullus today might be more likely to use an iPad than its precursor the *codicillus* (an erasable wax tablet). Yet, though technology has changed immeasurably, the human heart remains a lonely hunter.

> *This is one of those views which are so absurd that only very learned men could possibly adopt them.* (Bertrand Russell)

Holzberg's main points (pp. 35-36) on the otherness of ancient Roman sexual conceptualization are addressed *seriatim:*

> Roman sexual ideology did not see masculinity as a biolological state, but as something that had to be earned and

that could be forfeited again at any time.

As recently as January 14, 2011, *avant garde* artist Geoffrey Chadsey comments in an interview: "I heard a quote today, from someone who could not attribute the source, that goes 'women are, men become'."[80] Not much in the way of 'otherness', in that respect, between then and now.

> Only when a free Roman male – and personal liberty was one prerequisite for the attainment of masculinity – could wield a certain kind of power as head of a household, landowner, politician, soldier, etc., would he reach the status of a man.

Is that, in any essential way, different from the attitudes of today?

> The males classified as unmanly included, on the other hand, boys, especially boys who were the object of male sexual desires, and adult men who took the passive role in male-to-male relationships, but also all ailing, infirm, and old men ...

Again, there is no important difference in how relative degrees of manliness are viewed today.

> ... and even adulterers, whose lack of sexual discipline meant, according to prevailing opinion, that they lacked self-control.

How often have we seen contemporary politicians ruin their career because of marital infidelity? To the extent that masculinity, then and now, is measured in part by a man's degree of self-control, marital infidelity cannot but be viewed as less than fully manly.[81]

Holzberg continues:

> Sexual relationships were therefore not so much a question of gender differences, but of power structures. The distinction made was not really between male and female, certainly not between heterosexual and homosexual, but between those who had power and those who had none, between active and passive.

Wiseman (1987, p. 10), as a strong proponent of the other-ness of ancient Rome, concurs:

> The question 'Was Catullus homosexual?' could not have been asked by his contemporaries, because their termi-nology – and therefore also, we assume, their conceptual framework – was quite different from that of the twentieth century. The words 'homosexual' and 'heterosexual' were unknown even in the English language before Krafft-Ebing and Havelock Ellis; their etymology is 'barbarously hybrid', as Ellis himself observed in 1897, and the con-cepts they express are neither Greek nor Roman. The an-cients evidently did not find it helpful to categorise sexual activity according to the sex of the person with whom it is performed. What mattered to them was the question of active or passive, of penetrating or being penetrated.

This set of assumptions, in Wiseman's words (regarding the not unrelated matter of what inferences the record warrants), "collapses upon close inspection." Indeed, it collapses upon *casual* inspection: In the cosmopolitan precincts of the con-temporary world, same-sex marriage is increasingly accepted by most people, particularly the young (and it is enthusiasti-cally embraced by commercial interests). Marriage *indifferent* to the respective genders of the marrying couple is quite rare in the context of the ancient Mediterranean world, and even then it is perceived in traditional biological terms.

Earnest Cary (p. 159) translates a relevant passage from Cassius Dio (*c.* 155 CE – post-229 CE):[82]

> Now Nero called Sporus "Sabina" not merely because, owing to his resemblance to her he had been made a eunuch, but because the boy, like the mistress ["Sabina" also], had been solemnly married to [Nero] in Greece, Tigellinus giving the bride [*sic*] away, as the law ordained. All the Greeks held a celebration in honour of their mar-riage, uttering all the customary good wishes, even to the extent of praying that legitimate children might be born to them. After that Nero had two bedfellows at once, Pythagoras to play the rôle of husband to him, and Sporus that of wife. The latter, in addition to other forms of address, was termed "lady," "queen," and "mistress."

This does not suggest gender-indifference in conceptualizing sexuality; nor that there is anything socially normative about same-sex unions, but rather that absolute power has absolute prerogatives.

What's in a Name?

> *What's in a name? That which we call a rose*
> *By any other name would smell as sweet.*
> (William Shakespeare)

That a gender-neutral word for same-sex preference, "homosexuality", or complementary-sex preference, "heterosexuality", does not appear before its usage in 19th century medical literature no more implies the prior absence of consciousness of such than does the relatively recent vintage of the medical terms "manic-depression" or "bipolar disorder". The only safe inference to be drawn is that it is not until the 19th century that the medical profession begins in earnest to adopt terminology free of moral stigma regarding human sexuality.

For example, the word "queer" first appears in the written record in 1508 xrl.us/bmguny. Its first *recorded* use as a pejorative for same-sex preference does not occur until 1812, but that does not preclude its earlier use as such in casual conversation. Naturally, such a value-laden term (or some other like it) would hardly be suitable for the medical literature of the Victorian Era. (*See* http://xrl.us/bngveb for more recent connotations of "queer".) Far from being "barbarous", the term "homosexual", though it carries the stigma of implied pathology, at least relieves the phenomenon of moral stigma.

Similarly, English contains a great many words for distinct colors. If verbal equivalents existed in ancient Latin, they have not survived. But, this does not imply that ancient Roman artists lack conscious awareness of them as distinct from colors for which they do have a specific word. The only safe inference to be drawn in this case, likewise, is that color does not become a subject of rigorous scientific inquiry, or commercial product differentiation, until recent centuries.

Holzberg proceeds:

Since penetration had absolute priority before all other practices in sexual relationships, it was simply a question of the penetrators on the one side and the penetrated on the other. To the first belonged only those who had control over others, who had control over themselves, who were active, and in this sense 'real men': the second group comprised all the rest – women of every social rank, boys, *viri molles* [<'pansies'>], and slaves.

Is that not how most of the people in today's world, in their heart of hearts, view the matter at its most basic? The major difference between the ancient Greeks and Romans on the one hand, and the contemporary West on the other, is that in the case of the former, adult males are granted more wiggle room, so to speak, to sexually exploit boys without losing their status as, using Holzberg's term, 'real men'.[83]

In the same passage, Holzberg interprets this phenomenon thus:

This clearly defined system meant for one thing that pederasty was not considered indecent, simply because the power distribution between the active man and the passive boy was in keeping with the norm.

Upon closer examination, though, this form of sexual exploitation is not as gender-indifferent as it might at first appear. The boys who are thus exploited – without risk of loss of manly status to the exploiter – are described as *beardless* youth. In other words, these youth are prepubescent, and thus have not yet crossed the threshold into *biological* manhood. In that sense, if readers would forgive this construction, beardless boys are surrogate 'girls'.

Thomson (2003, p. 250:4), commenting upon Carmen 16:4, indicates that Catullus's 'kiss' poems about Iuventius <"the Lad"> are what elicit ridicule from Catullus's literary frenemies Aurelius and Furius (conceivably, in now-lost song-poems of their own):

parum pudicum = *impudicum* [<sexual immodesty>]. The word is usually appropriated to homosexuality [*sic*]; hence it seems likely that the *milia multa basiorum* [<many thou-

sands of 'kisses'>] in l. 12 are those of poem 48, rather than of poems 5 and 7.

(As shall be seen, Holzberg thinks that song-poems 5 and 7 {the Lesbia 'kiss' poems} are the source of this literary feud.)

Dyson (Hejduk) tellingly observes (Skinner, ed., 2007, p. 268):

> The relationship between a man and an adolescent boy was characterized by its artificiality and temporariness: **once body hair took over, the relationship would end** (sex of any kind between adult men is the subject of disgust and ridicule in Roman poetry). [Emphasis added.]

Further, based upon general reading, my impression is that in contemporary cultures in which single men have far fewer opportunities for intimacy with women than in the West, a similar dispensation, partial or plenary, is afforded 'real men'. Even in the West, there seems to be a comparable dispensation among all-male prison populations.

Further still, in the Rome of that era, there are children exploited as workers in mines, women do not have political rights and have few economic ones, slavery is widespread and includes the brutality of gladiatorial "games" as a form of public entertainment. Together, these reflect a much more constrained view of human rights compared with today – not gender-indifference, as such, in sexual matters.

Judith P Hallett and Skinner, as editors of *Roman Sexualities*, present a compendium of scholarly articles of great breadth, depth, and insight. Hallett (pp. 257-8) states the matter thus:

> **By comparing Roman reactions to female and male same-sex love, I am assuming that Roman thought**, perhaps under the influence of the categoric constructions presented in ... Plato's *Symposium*, **regarded each as a distinct phenomenon and the two as relatively comparable and parallel phenomena. I do so on the basis of several Latin texts ....** I recognize that both classicists and modern historians have lately argued that the conceptualization of homosexual desire as a discrete phenomenon – that is, the categorization of sexual passion according to the gender of both the subject and

object choice – ranks as a recent development in medical thought. Inasmuch as the medical authorities (such as Havelock Ellis) who promulgate this view of homosexual desire write extensively about classical texts and topics, I would regard ancient authors such as those we will survey as a major source of this late nineteenth- and early twentieth-century scientific conceptualization. [Emphasis added.]

In other words, ancient Romans view this matter in the same way as do the vast majority of people in the modern world: There are those who have a same-sex preference, and there are those who do not. The only people who have a greatly different viewpoint are Ellis and those relative few (compared with the whole of contemporary humanity) who share his perspective.

Unfortunately, from the standpoint of cosmopolitan values of tolerance and inclusiveness, the Latin texts that Hallett presents reflect a view of same-sex preference little, if at all, different from the most rank homophobia of today. Obloquy is heaped upon those men who are perceived as 'feminine', and upon those women who are perceived as 'masculine'. Certainly in ancient times, effeminacy and masculinity are understood as grounded in biology, rather than arising from social determinants – as Hallett's examples clearly show.

Hallett begins her article (pp. 255-56) with the text, and her translation, of a poem by the fabulist Phaedrus (*c*. 15 BCE - *c*. 50 CE) concerning why some women prefer intimacy with women in the manner more typical of men and, *vis-à-vis* men, *vice versa:* Prometheus, the mythic Greek Titan who creates humankind, becomes inebriated while attending a party hosted by Bacchus, God of wine, song, and attendant merriment. After stumbling home late at night, Prometheus assigns a male sex organ to certain women, and its complement to certain men.

Noting that Phaedrus uses a Latin word of Greek origin that means to rub, *tribas*, to indicate what in contemporary slang might be called a woman who is 'butch', and that the mythic Prometheus is also of Greek origin, Hallett surmises from this and a poem fragment that precedes it:

... [T]he contexts of the two poems, inasmuch as both are surrounded by avowedly fictitious representations of talking animals, do not foster the impression that either features contemporary and actual human phenomena. Indeed, by crediting the origin of *tribades* to a Greek figure from the remote past, Phaedrus further dissociates females who engage in same-sex love from the actual and contemporary human scene. What is more, the implication that tribads actually possess male organs (presumably on their groins as well as in their mouths) serves to distance them even more from any claim to present-day Roman reality.

Hallett (p. 256) presents, and translates, the preceding fragment, thus:

formavit recens
a fictione veretri linguam mulieris
adfinitatem traxit inde obscenitas (Phaedrus, *Fabulae*
4.14 xrl.us/bmgssz)

Lately he formed the tongue of woman from the molding
of the male organ.
From this source obscenity has attracted a bond of
kinship by marriage.

Hallett observes:

[This fragment] also apparently attributes to Prometheus the origin of another contemporary and actual human phenomenon, the female tongue; in this earlier fragment Phaedrus provides an equally implausible source (the male organ) and a similarly censorious assessment of its impact.

That is a defensible reading. Yet, Phaedrus's fragmentary fable may be read as both more and less than that. Another rendering of Phaedrus's shorter fragment might be:

Recently he fashioned
the tongue of woman in the form of the penis.
Thenceforth, it conveyed obscenity.

Note that what Phaedrus characterizes as *obscenitas* is, again, based in biological analogy, not in the violation of social norms.

As well, Phaedrus may be using *obscenitas* in an ironic sense; if so, he would not be the only humorist who mocks the shock felt by those less liberal in such matters.

Phaedrus is explicit that his fables are no more than such. Yet, it is clear from these verses that the underlying concept of same-sex preference is entirely biological.

Hallett (p. 257) notes that Phaedrus employs as progenitor of same-sex preference a figure from Greek mythology (Prometheus), a Frankenstein-lab mixup of sex organs, and a Greek rooted word, *tribas*, for what might today be called a Lesbian 'top'. She concludes from this (and other examples from Latin literature) that, in marked contrast to the treatment the subject receives in Plato's *Symposium*, Romans viewed female same-sex couplings as:

> ...a Greek practice, geographically and chronologically distanced from present-day Roman behavior, and as abnormal and unreal, involving the use and possession of male sexual apparatus.

Another interpretation might be that, unlike the philosopher Plato who is trying to *educate* his readers, the fabulist Phaedrus is merely trying to *entertain* them. Phaedrus may only be suggesting that the female tongue is not so much *constructed* from the male sex organ as it is *shaped* in such a way as to serve as an approximate substitute for same in certain contexts.[84] Additionally, Phaedrus imputes an anatomical complementarity on the part of *molles mares* <male 'softies'>.

To this day, "Greek" is sometimes used as a shorthand for genital-anal sex. "Tribbing" is a contemporary slang term for genital-genital rubbing by female partners. I have been personal witness, in an informal social setting, to one female acquaintance loudly exclaiming to another (half indignantly, half in jest): "Suck my *dick!*" – several times, as the evening wore on. I do not think that any of these examples indicate a temporal, geographical, or cultural distancing from the here and now, or a misunderstanding of human anatomy. The most enlightened thinking of today is that same-sex preference is biologically determined. The ancient Romans, however pejorative their judgment of the matter and however imprecise their medical metaphors, seem to agree.

Space is not available to do justice to the acuity and nuance of Hallett's analysis. I highly recommend it to anyone interested in how male Roman authors (unfortunately, female voices have not survived) treat the phenomenon of female same-sex preference and practice (including sympathetic treatments by Ovid and {the otherwise often cynical} Juvenal).

Support for Hallett's line of reasoning can be found in modern journalism's seemingly inexhaustible enthusiasm for employing the word "Mafia" to characterize any form of ongoing criminal activity – by anyone, anywhere, at any time. It routinely is used even in non-criminal contexts, such as "Hyannis Port Mafia" (associates of Senator Edward Kennedy), "Memphis Mafia" (associates of Elvis), *etc.* Continuing the analogy: There are many fables associated with the Mafia that no skeptical reader can believe are true.[85]

This is indeed a distancing tool, implying that such people and their behavior are characteristic of *them* – not *us* (ie, the author and the author's core readership). In other words, I *hear* Hallett on her point. *My* point is that, taken as a whole, Hallett's article reveals beyond reasonable argument that the view of human sexuality in ancient Rome is fraught with much emotion, danger, misinformation that is sometimes patently ridiculous, gender bias, contradiction, confusion, controversy, and blatant hypocrisy – just as it is everywhere *today*.

In sum, my view of the proposition that ancient Romans conceptualized sexuality in ways greatly unlike our own is: Case not proven.

How 'Lesbian' Is Lesbia?

Holzberg's reading of "Lesbia" as an artfully imagined *hetaera* does liberate him from his bourgeois diffidence regarding the well-born 'Mrs Metelli'.[86] He thus dispels the notion that Catullus's choice of the pseudonym "Lesbia" is entirely innocent of sexual connotation. Wiseman (1987, p. 135), though it is contrary to his overall verdict of 'not guilty',[87] concedes that by Catullus's time the word *lesbia* itself, along with various compounds, already has been for centuries inextricably associated with oral sex – albeit hilariously androcentric in perspective (in the surviving record at least).

As best as I can reconstruct the 'male logic' of the matter (if 'logic' is the right word): The Island of Lesbos has conducted religious rites to women's beauty, *kallisteia*, since before the time of Homer, and might still be doing so in Catullus's day. Hence, "Lesbos was traditionally associated with refinement and sophistication, for example in music, poetry and dress" (Wiseman, *ibid*). Sappho writes poetry about beauty gene-rally, and beautiful women particularly. She also writes refin-ed poetry of her love for women. Women loving women is a social taboo. Fellating a man is also a social taboo. Therefore (from the male point of view): Lesbians love to fellate men[!]

It bears noting, though, that both Wiseman and Holzberg cite the Alexandrian *comic stage* as the source for this counter-intuitive concept of Lesbian desire. The comic stage of the time, like the television 'sitcoms' of more recent times, offers its audience that which allows them to laugh aloud in public at their shared discomfit about subjects they normally keep private. For a contemporary equivalent of the subtlety of these offerings, think *Hustler* magazine. It is possible, then, that the comics are, perhaps analogously to television's *The Colbert Report*, just *joking* – the joke being the absurdity of men thinking Lesbians have a preference for performing oral sex for the pleasure of *men*.[88]

Whatever (male) authors of that era may have understood to be the essence of Lesbian desire, Clodia/Lesbia's idea of having a good time is suggested by both Cicero and Catullus. Cicero's naughty pun on Clodia's peds is presented in n. 52 below. To this may be added the clear in its implication disdain Cicero expresses on a number of occasions for the oral 'uncleanliness' of Clodius's henchman and scribe, Sex-tus Cloelius (a slave whom Clodius may have purchased dur-ing his Quaestership of Sicily).

Two of these denunciations of Cloelius's lack of 'oral hygiene' are made with regard to Clodia. Shortly after Cicero's return from exile, he delivers an oration arguing that he has not been adequately recompensed for the loss of his home brought about by Clodius during Cicero's exile. (Cloelius may have personally supervised the pillage and destruction of Cicero's properties.) The oration becomes an occasion for Cicero to make collateral attacks on the allegedly gross mismanagement of Clodius's legislation providing free grain for Rome's poor:

> *scilicet tu helluoni spurcatissimo praegustatori libidinum tuarum homini egentissimo et facinerosissimo sex clodio socio tui sanguinis qui sua lingua etiam sororem tuam a te abalienavit* (*De Domo Sua* 25 <u>xrl.us/bihd7s</u>)

> Naturally, you [gave control of the granaries] to the filthiest pig, the 'pre-taster' of your lusts, the most greedy and corrupt of men, *Sextus Cloelius*, your 'friend of the family' who with his own tongue actually *pried* your sister from you.

Regarding Cloelius's non-appearance that day, Cicero snarks:

> *si requiri iusseris invenient hominem apud sororem tuam occultantem se capite demisso* (*De Domo Sua* 83 <u>xrl.us/b mgp4j</u>)

> If you were to order a search, they will come upon the man at your sister's – hiding by giving her head.

Commenting upon these passages, Wiseman (1987, p. 41) perceptively observes about Cloelius's relationship to Clodia what might equally apply to Catullus's:

> What Cicero alleges – though not, of course, in so many words – is that Cloelius too was Clodia's lover, or at least the instrument of her pleasure. We cannot know what truth there was in the allegation, but the type of intercourse to which Cicero alludes would indeed be appropriate to their respective statuses – she the wilful and imperious mistress, he the dependant who must gratify her wish, whatever the humiliation to himself.

You must remember this –
A kiss is still a kiss ... (Herman Hupfeld)

Is a 'Kiss' Still a Kiss?

Holzberg (p. 42) proposes that in *Carmen* 5 Catullus employs for kisses the atypical words (perhaps of rustic origin) *basia* (5:7) and *basiorum* (5:13) because he is asking Lesbia for 'kisses' (by the many hundreds and thousands) that are not of the ordinary sort. In *Carmen* 7, Lesbia wants to know how many of these special kisses – *basiationes* (7:1), *basia multa basiare* (7:9) – would *satisfy* Catullus?

Catullus answers: The number of sands of Libya and stars in the sky will do.

Holzberg suggests this may indicate Catullus's (imagined?) inability to achieve penetration. Hence, Holzberg asks, "Does not a woman who has just been addressed as Lesbia for the first time seem eminently suitable as a therapist?" (Thus, by implication, Holzberg pathologizes the etiology of avidness for oral sex.)

According to Holzberg, because Catullus has received so many such 'kisses' from *Clodia* (cp. Thomson, pp. 59-60 above), implying penetrative incapacity, his (imaginary?) friends Aurelius and Furius question Catullus's manhood. Catullus replies in *Carmen* 16 that Aurelius is a 'pansy' who will be 'kissing' *him*, and Furius's own 'poofter' *derriere* is going to be receiving a vivid demonstration of Catullus's penetrative capability.

In this vein, Holzberg might have noted (were it not inconvenient for his premise) that in *Carmen* 48 (which regards Catullus's crush on Iuventius), *basiare* (48:2) and *basiem* (48:3) also appear (in this case, a mere *milia ... trecenta* <300,000> 'kisses'). And, the last word of this song-poem is *osculationis*, which in context strongly suggest 'kisses' of a certain sort.[89]

The only other surviving usage of the latter Latin word appears in *Pro Caelio* (49 xrl.us/bmfcbz) as *osculatione*, in which passage Cicero is fulminating about Clodia's outrageous (to Cicero, at least) *public* behavior at beach parties and boat parties. Again, the context requires that these 'kisses' be other than a mere peck on the cheek. (It would be interesting to learn whether the orator borrowed this coinage from the song-poet or *vice versa,* or if both took it from a now-lost earlier source.)

Helpfully, Holzberg (p. 41, with cites to several other scholars) points out that *glubit* <peels, *eg,* an ear of corn; here, apparently, foreskins)> (58:5) has a relevant onomatopoetic quality to it.

Holzberg concludes his article (p. 43) by remarking that it is possible that *basia* as "'kissification' in Catullus's day could be taken to mean *fellatio* by those who wanted to see it that way ..."

I have yet to encounter a suggestion, though, that *basia* may imply Catullus's oral attentions on behalf of Clodia/Lesbia. To those similarly inclined, the *passer* <sp*arrow*> of 2:1 xrl.us/bm3g82 and 3:3-4/15-16 xrl.us/bmfebk may have as one of its allusive referents a complementary portion of *Lesbia's* anatomy. My Catullus does not 'do' *innocent* coincidence. Consider the slew of sibilants in Carmen 5 xrl.us/b mfftg. The reader is invited to imagine Catullus reciting this to Clodia in a stage whisper, with exaggerated lisp. Note the resultant movement of his tongue, especially as he lingers over *Lesbia, basia,* and *basiorum.*[90]

In sum, it may be that the Sappho/Lesbia nexus includes a shared preference for a lover's oral attentions, whichever the lover's gender. If so, Catullus's sobriquet "Lesbia" would indeed be teasing, but it would also be an acknowledgment of her status as his *Domina.*

Why Can't a Woman Be More Like a Man?[91]

Rumor has it that Caesar is *omnium mulierum virum et omnium virorum mulierem* <every woman's *husband,* and every man's *wife*>. (Suetonius, *Vita Divi Iuli* 52 xrl.us/bicvoa)

I have read assertions that this is no more than political invective. But, I have not read it argued that a *male* member of the august Iulian line, *per se,* would not have behaved in such a manner. Nor have I read it argued that Clodius, solely by virtue of being a member of the *gens* <clan> Claudii, would not have behaved as Cicero charges. In spite of, or *because* of, her own august lineage, why could not Clodia/Lesbia behave however she might please?

Ironically, what seems to underlie *au currant* assertions that Clodia Metelli is not as *Pro Caelio* portrays her, nor as Catullus portrays Lesbia (in Holzberg's reading, does not even *exist*) is a variation on the old-fashioned Madonna/Whore bifurcation of women: more precisely in this case, *either* "a female member of the senatorial class" (*see* n. 86 below) *or* a *hetaera* – who perhaps bears some resemblance to a freed slave of Catullus's acquaintance.

This presumes that the two roles are mutually exclusive. While that is (often) true in the literal sense, it should be obvious, certainly to anyone who reads poetry, that *le cœur a ses raisons que la raison ne connaît point* <the heart has its reasons the point of which the mind is ignorant>.

More ironic still is that Holzberg's revisionist reading, and its variants, argue that the conformity of Cicero's *Pro Caelio* and Catullus's *carmina* to the prevailing stereotypes about women in that era demonstrates that their portraits of Clodia/ Lesbia are no more than male fantasies. Yet, why would *contemporaneous* stereotypes of women be any more distorting of Cicero's and Catullus's account of a woman they both know personally (whether she be aristocrat or freed slave) than are *contemporary* stereotypes about two Roman men we know only by their surviving documents from 2,000 years earlier? In other words, who/whom is viewing these issues through the distorting lens of stereotypes?

Are there not women who in the most private place of their heart feel themselves to be *both* Madonna *and* meretrix? By the same token, are there not men who, their embarrassing reality notwithstanding, secretly feel that they are 'Caesar' (ironically so, since the historical Caesar's reputation falls well short of the stereotypical masculine ideal)?

Sapphic Mistress: The Great Mother

The irony continues (Holzberg, p. 33):

In the *communis opinio* [<consensus>] of Catullan scholars, however, the idea of a hetaera being the object of the *poeta/amator*'s [<love-poet's>] love is barely even a remote possibility as acceptable basis for interpretation. On the contrary: the very name Lesbia is widely perceived as a sign of the poet's romantic idealization of his *puella*, because it is read as an allusion to the poetess Sappho from the island of Lesbos .... Catullan scholars therefore see Lesbia not only as a lady from one of Rome's noble families, but also as the Muse who inspires Catullus, and as the *puella docta* [<in Holzberg's context: cultivated Mistress>] who can fully appreciate his poetry .... In Catullus's texts, however, there is absolutely no trace of this Lesbia the Sapphic Muse and *puella docta*, not even an implicit shadow [followed by citations to other scholars who share his misreading of *Carmen* 35] .... What the texts do offer is, by contrast, a clear case for deriving their Lesbia from, amongst other things, λεσβιάζειν [<*lesbiazein*>], a Greek word for *fellare* .... For those who tread the biographical path to Catullus, the idea is, of course, scarcely compa-tible with Lesbia the projected sublime, Sapphic [M]use.

(Perhaps, comprehending certain matters requires having been there.[92])

Thus, Holzberg criticizes colleagues who read Catullus's song-poems as versified reflections on his affair with "a lady from one of Rome's noble families" who is "the [M]use who inspires Catullus, and ... the *puella docta* who can fully appreciate his poetry", because it prevents them from viewing Lesbia as an imaginary *hetaera*.

But, is that not *precisely* the role of the *hetaera*? Green (2005, p. 8) observes:

> Young men sought an outlet for their more unruly passions – and **often for intellectual or artistic companionship** as well ... from the world of call-girls and demi-mondaines which, as always, was not slow to spring up in response to a steady demand .... Eastern campaigns ... imported exotic attractions in the form of Greek-educated musicians, dancers, and **high-class literary call-girls** whose sexual favors – at a price – were packaged with

cultural trimmings, and **who often entered into long-term relationships with their clients** ... [Emphasis added; cp. Woody Allen, "The Whore of Mensa" <u>bit.ly/IQnUn</u>.]

To support his view that a woman given the pseudonym "Lesbia" (thus, to Holzberg, a *fellatrix*) would not be capable of being a love-poet's sublime Sapphic Muse, Holzberg makes the yet-more ironic claim mid-paragraph: "In Catullus's texts, however, there is absolutely no trace of this Lesbia the Sapphic Muse and *puella docta* ..."; ironic because in doing so he dismissively references the very text that disproves his assertion, *Carmen* 35 <u>xrl.us/bmfb35</u>:

> *ignosco tibi sapphica puella*
> *musa doctior est enim venuste*
> *magna caecilio incohata mater* (16-18)

> I don't blame you, Sapphic Mistress
> more knowing than a Muse – it is indeed erotic:
> the Great Mother hasn't *finished* with *Caecilius!*

Carmen 35 will be discussed at some length in the forthcoming biography of Clodia. For our purposes here, as briefly as possible: For centuries song-poem 35 has been viewed as an innocent social invitation from Catullus to a fellow song-poet, named "Caecilius". Then Copley's 1953 article "Catullus 35" opens a sluice, unleashing a small but steady stream of articles asserting that 35 is a poem about *poetry*; specifically, Catullus's effort to tutor a younger song-poet.

A minority of voices, going back more than a century, have speculated that 35 refers to erotic intrigue, but their readings do not connect all the dots. It is not until *2006* that *sapphica puella* is first identified, by David Kutzko, as Lesbia. (Given the association of Sappho with the Island of *Lesbos*, who else could she possibly be but *Lesbia?*) Yet, Kutzko fails to realize that the *puella* who is Lesbia in 35:16 must therefore be the *puella* of 35:8. Kutzko instead reads *two puellae* (yet another counterproductive multiplication of entities), with the other of whom Lesbia is contrasted unfavorably.

And, he is unaware that this (nowhere-else-attested, save *Carmina* 67) song-poet, Caecilius (II), is the new "Caecilius" in Clodia/Lesbia's life.

Kutzko (p. 10) concludes: "Catullus' presentation of himself in Poem 35 and elsewhere – critical of others yet ultimately self-revealing – presages the first-person persona of elegy."

While that conclusion may be true from the standpoint of literary theory, Kutzko's reading, and that of every other commentator, fails to recognize the interpretation most consistent with the sense of the rest of the Catullan *oeuvre:* Catullus (35:1) mockingly refers to Caecilius II as *tenero poetae meo sodalis* <touching poet, my 'comrade' [in ClubClodia]>, *warning* him, based upon what Catullus hears has been said by 'Mr Cogitations' (*ie,* Cicero in *Pro Caelio* [93]) that Caecilius II better flee Clodia's impassioned embrace and her entreaties that he remain behind in New Como, and instead 'devour the way' to Catullus's side in Verona – rather than, by implication, devouring the 'canolis' Clodia fed Caecilius I (resulting in his death by poisoning, as implied by Cicero in *Pro Caelio* 59 xrl.us/bki59b).

Most daunting of all, Clodia/Lesbia has been *very* aroused sexually by reading a draft of Catullus's *Carmen* 63 xrl.us/bmfciy – possibly the most psychologically harrowing poem ever written (at least from a male point of view), certainly in Latin. Song-poem 63 versifies the travails of the *autocastrato* Attis, a *devotee* of *Magna Mater* <The Great Mother>, Goddess Cybele, whose connection to Clodia is alluded-to by Cicero in *Pro Caelio* 34, and whose festival is being celebrated the very day Cicero delivers this oration (*Pro Caelio* 1).

In Catullus's version of the legend, the handsome young Attis castrates himself with a flint knife (suggesting neolithic roots of this ritual), in accordance with the real-life rites by worshippers of the Great Mother, who, legendarily, resides among the wilds of Dindymus (thus Catullus refers to *Carmen* 63 as *The Dindymian Domina*). The next morning, Attis (now referenced with feminine pronouns) feels devastating remorse. 'She' attempts to flee, but the Great Mother reins her back in (using trained lions). Hence, she will spend the rest of her days enslaved to the Great Mother. Song-poem 63 concludes with Catullus begging the Great Mother to spare *him.*

In turn, Catullus ends song-poem 35 by tauntingly informing Caecilius II that the 'Great Mother' (by allusion, Clodia/Lesbia) is likewise *unfinished* with *him*.

By contrast, Thomson (1967, p. 227), interpreting Catullus's 'thank-you note' to Cicero (*Carmen* 49) as implicit *literary criticism* of Cicero's attempts at poetry, offers in support thereof this gloss of song-poem 35:

> This kind of diplomacy in the service of critical honesty can be found in Poem 35:
>
> "Caecilius, your work is *uenustus* [<erotic, but refined>] but really not quite finished, and a letter from a mutual friend confirms my view about this. So come quickly and hear about it. Oh, I know that girl fell in love with you at a first reading of the poem – and sure enough, she has taste, as you say; but really, it's not quite finished – anyway, come and hear what's still to be done to improve it". Thus Catullus – proceeding with care, in the prickly undergrowth of literary vanity.

However, I might translate *Carmen* 35 so:

> Power Mac, pray tell *mon confrère*,
> the 'sensitive poet' Caecilius:
> Hurry to Verona, forsaking the walls of
> New Como and the shore of Lake Como –
> for I want him to hear the cogitations
> of a certain 'friend' of his and mine.
> If he'll be smart, he'll devour the way,
> though his lady fair issue recalls by the thousands,
> throwing both hands around his neck,
> begging him to stay.
>
> She who now, if what's been confided in me be true,
> is dying from his impotence in *amore*.
> For, when she read the unfinished
> *Dindymian Domina*, since then the poor girl
> has been consumed by a fire inside her loins.
> I don't blame you, Sapphic Mistress,
> more knowing than a Muse – g
> The 'Great Mother' is surely
> *unfinished* with *Caecilius*!

Taking a cue from Thomson, my own between-the-lines reading could be expressed thus:

> Power Mac, tell Caecilius, wussy 'poet', latest member of Lake Como's ClubClodia, to leave her arms and charms, to ignore her entreaties, to come here to Verona, to come hear the deep thoughts of our good friend *Signore Cogitazioni*. (I owe him a thank-you note for leaving my name out of his masterpiece, *Pro Caelio*.) If Caecilius knows what's good for him, he'll gobble down the cobblestones along the way (rather than Clodia's canopés).

> Ah Clodia, the sunshine girl, has been aflame with romantic *ardour* ever since she read my *pièce de résistance* (a work still in progress). It's my take on the story of Attis and Goddess Cybele, the Great Mother.

> Sapphic Clodia: *you* know Goddess Cybele – she whose monument was on a Rome-bound ship that ran aground. It could only be dislodged by an ancestress of *yours* (her own virtue til then much in question).

> Indeed, the annual festival and games in Goddess Cybele's honor, the Megalenses, are also the occasion of (my former 'best friend forever') Caelius's trial in the Roman Forum – the one in which you, of all people, accuse *him* of trying to poison *you!*

> (Speaking of 'the Great Mother', how about the way Clodia's daughter Metella is turning out! Like mother – like daughter, they say. But then, allowances must be made because Metella's father (her mother's *previous* Caecilius) died so *suddenly*, while the girl was still in her formative years – indeed, the very year New Como was founded.)

> However, *poetry* is what is really on my mind. My just-begun yet almost-finished poem, *The Dindymian Domina/ Great Mother*, puts a bit of a different spin on the story of Cybele and Attis: Instead of Cybele falling in love with Attis – and he castrating himself to expiate his guilt for subsequently cheating on her – this new, improved Attis *preemptively* castrates himself (with a flint-stone knife – ouch!) as a mere *token* of his devotion to the Great Mother, and as penance for male offenses against women

generally. The morning after, s/he does entertain certain 'cogitations' of her/his own about this rash excision (but, alas, too late). S/he even tries to make good an escape from the Great Mother's clutches. But, as they also say, Mother knows best, and s/he is soon brought back into line.

Poor girl: Is it any wonder that you, Clodia – Sapphic Mistress more knowing than a Muse – would be inflamed with *ardour* by such a storyline? Ah, yes, the 'Great Mother' is just-begun/unfinished – with *Caecilius!*

In sum: I do not know how Catullus could be more clear that Clodia/Lesbia is his Sapphic Muse, as both *matrona* and *hetaera*.

> *It's still the same old story –*
> *A fight for love and glory ...* (Herman Hupfeld)

Has there never been a poet who falls madly in love with a wealthy well-born patroness who, for a time, indulges that poet's need for an eroticized mother-figure (or, "therapist" in Holzberg's analogy), and then moves on to other 'puppies', much to the poet's disillusionment and bitter disappointment? Has there never been a poet who versified his experience of such?

Is the poet who writes to his beloved in his (apparently) final words to her:

> *nec meum respectet ut ante amorem*
> *qui illius culpa cecidit velut prati*
> *ultimi flos praetereunte postquam*
> *tactus aratro est* (11:21-24)

Do not look again, as before, for my love,
which you casually castrated
like a flower at a meadow's edge –
sliced by a passing plough.

... merely effecting a literary *topos* about an imaginary *hetaera?* Perhaps so – but, it's not the way *my* Catullus walked.

Hammer and Siècle

More broadly, what seems to underlie a trend in the literary scholarship of recent decades can be summed up in the homely adage: To a hammer, everything looks like a nail. By analogy, for a good many philologists, literary works tend to look like nothing *other* than literary scholarship.

Though the essence of high culture is the increasing refinement of sense and sensibility, if works of art are *only* the refinement of perception of other artwork, we are left with mirrors held up to mirrors, rather than to life itself.

Admittedly, the mirror the artist holds up to life is a distorted one. Unlike the literary and performing arts, life does not always have a 'plot' with a tidy ending – comical in popular entertainment, tragic in more rarefied offerings. Yet, just as surely, art (at least that which will be long remembered) is mirroring *something* about real life – other than art itself.[94]

Hejduk (p. 6) sensibly remarks: "[Catullus] must have had some sort of involvement with Lesbia's model (if it were pure fiction he would be a laughingstock)."

Green (2005, p. 5) points out:

> [O]ne of the instantly observable phenomena of Greek and Roman culture is that original invention, out of whole cloth as it were, in both cases came late and with difficulty. The tendency was always – certainly was still in Catullus's day – to work from life.

From the viewpoint of poetic sense, Elmer Truesdell Merrill (p. xxiv) xrl.us/bk6wpm states categorically: "That we have in the poems of Catullus a real and not an imaginative sketch of a love-episode cannot be once doubted by him who reads."

Whenever possible, substitute constructions out of known entities for inferences to unknown entities. (Bertrand Russell)

- If Lesbia has no real-life correlate in "Clodia", why does Apuleius cite her as such in defending his own use of pseudonyms for real people in his writings? If Apuleius is referring to one of Clodia Metelli's sisters, where is credible evidence that *either* sister has changed her birth name from *Claudia* to *Clodia?* (*See* Appendix D.)

- If Lesbia bears no more than a faint resemblance to a freed slave of Catullus's acquaintance who happens to be named "Clodia", why does Catullus hide *her* real identity behind a pseudonym – yet viciously attack the likes of *Caesar* by *his* real name?

- Where is the evidence that either of Clodia Metelli's sisters is married at a time when Catullus is already old enough to begin an adulterous affair?

- Where is the evidence that a "Caelius" or a "Rufus" has an affair with either of Clodia Metelli's sisters?

- Whether sarcastic or sincere, what can song-poem 49 possibly mean – with its obvious 'quotations' from his own *Carmen* 36 and from Cicero's *Pro Caelio* – if not that Catullus's *puella* is Cicero's *Clodia Metelli?*

- If Cicero's *Pro Caelio* is the dishonest sliming of the innocent widow of an esteemed colleague of the Jurists themselves, why is not Cicero run out of Rome on a rail (permanently, this time) – as *any* attorney would be in like circumstances?

- If Catullus is merely 'riffing' on existing literary motifs, why is he savaging friends (and/or their relatives), not to mention *Caesar* and *Mamurra*, by name?

- If *Caelius Rufus* did not know Catullus in Verona when both were young, why does Catullus not give this *other* *Caelius* a pseudonym?

- If the second prosecutor of Caelius is a *P Clodius* other than Clodia's *brother*, why does Cicero style his name exactly as he does the name of Clodia's brother many times in his other writings, including private correspondence?

- If Catullus's poems hostile to Clodia are merely versifications of Cicero's accusations in *Pro Caelio*, which of Cicero's orations are being versified in Catullus's other hostile poems?

Commentators and other readers alike are free to extract from the source documents whatever meaning may make the most sense to them. It happens, though, that the most *unambiguous* reading is that Clodia Metelli is substantially as Cicero describes her, whatever liberties he may have taken as a defense attorney, and that she is Catullus's *Lesbia,* whatever poetic liberties he may have taken. This reading best fits the documents, requires the fewest extra-documentary assumptions, and raises the fewest unanswerable questions.

From the perspective of poetic sense, the identification of *Lesbia* as Clodia Metelli further illustrates Catullus's artistic brilliance: If *Lesbia* is Clodia Metelli, the *Caecilius carmina* (35 and 67), the *Rufus carmina* (69 and 77), the *Caelius carmina* (58 and 100), the *Marcus Tullius carmen* (49), and the *Cornelius carmina* (1, 67, and 102 {*see* Appendix E}) together form a fascinating mosaic-in-verse, with Clodia Metelli at its aesthetic center (and 67 near the numerical center of the 116-poem corpus). If *Lesbia* is *not* Clodia Metelli, then Catullus has merely created a pile of unrelated 'tiles' – *and failed to recognize the most obvious reading of his own poems.*

Ergo, *Lesbia* is beyond (reasonable) doubt the real-life Clodia Metelli, the knowing Sapphic Muse whom Catullus loved, lost, and, as a result thereof, launched them both into literary immortality. Unless Catullus were to abandon the use of a pseudonym entirely, I do not know how he could make more apparent this identification. The scholarly consensus that this identification cannot be made with absolute certainty demonstrates that Catullus's *objective* in using a pseudonym for Clodia has been successful all along. *QED.*

If it is further accepted that Catullus is more interested in immortalizing himself by writing about *Clodia* than in disseminating to a Roman audience mere slave-girl gossip regarding otherwise obscure figures from Brescia and Verona, then it is obvious who is the 'mystery woman' of *Carmen* 67.

To 'Get' Catullus: Begin at the End; End at the Beginning

Catullus wrote at least two dozen song-poems about a woman he calls *Lesbia* in 13 of them. As discussed, though never using her real name, Catullus leaves a number of clues that point listeners, or later readers, in the direction of Clodia Metelli. And, Catullus is wont to insert his 'punch-line' into a song-poem's final verse or verses (Copley 1953, p.152).

Thus, when reading a Catullan song-poem that focuses on an unnamed and unusually free-spirited woman, I first ask myself: Is the woman *Clodia?* If the final verse or verses suggest that the woman *is* Clodia (*eg, Carmina* 17 xrl.us/bmfb3x, 35, and the present one), I assume this to be the case, unless and until proven otherwise.

This assumption leads me to view debates over *voto* vs *gnato* (67:5), *est* vs *es* and *facta* vs *pacta* (67:6), *vobis* vs *nobis* (67: 7), *Chinea* vs *Cycneae* (67:32), *praecurrit* vs *procurrit* (67:33), *etc*, as subsidiary issues, lest the *anus* wag the *canus*. Whatever the correct taxonomy of this-or-that 'leaf' on the Catullan landscape, the 'forest' is Clodia.

The Final Four – The End of the Affair

The last four verses of song-poem 67 (45-48) are 'spoken' by the Door:

> *praeterea addebat quendam quem dicere nolo*
> *nomine ne tollat rubra supercilia*
> *longus homo est magnas cui lites intulit olim*
> *falsum mendaci ventre puerperium*

She added *en passant* a certain someone whose name
I don't want to say, lest he *arch* russet eyebrows.
He's a tall man who at one time made major arguments
against a *belly of lies* over a *miscarried* boy-birth!

Copley's understanding of what a coherent reading of this song-poem *requires* is, in my view, precisely on point (1949, p. 245):

> [Editors' and students'] collective efforts may be found in several articles and in almost any modern commentary on Catullus.[1] ..... **The poem, by its very nature, has to have a simple solution.**[2] It is a *diffamatio*, a lampoon; its purpose is to defame and ridicule. Passing from hand to hand, circulating through the *convivia* [<dinner parties>], **it was to be read and digested at a glance**, for only so would it cause laughter, and only if it caused

laughter, would it achieve its intended aim. **People do not laugh at a poem which needs a commentary to be understood**; yet if the poem means what modern scholarship has tried to make it mean, Catullus' own contemporaries would have needed the services of some earlier-day Kroll or Ellis to enable them to see its point.

Actually, the poem is not a riddle at all. It tells a simple, straightforward, and not very pretty tale of adultery and cuckoldry, involving a man, his son, the son's wife, and the wife's various lovers. **The only "riddle" in the poem is the identity of the unnamed "Man with Red Hair" who figures in the concluding lines (43-48)**, but this is a riddle only to us of a latter day. **We may be certain that Catullus' contemporaries knew at once who the redhaired man was.** [Emphasis added.]

1 E.g. R. Cahen, *RPh* 26 (1902) 164-180; W. Kroll, *Philologus* 63 (1904) 139-147; H. Magnus. *Phillogus* 66 (1907) 296-312; G. Per[r]otta. *Athenaeum* N.S. 5-6 (1927-28) 160-190.
2 Per[r]otta admits this (*op. cit.,* 161), as does Magnus (*op. cit.,* 296), but their solutions are as confusing and complex as the others.

Indeed, I too, more than two thousand years later, (naively) realized "at a glance ..... at once who the redhaired man was." And yet, of this unnamed man, Green (2005, p. 250; cf. p. 45 above) posits: "[T]he tall ginger-eyebrowed fellow [is] not, certainly, Rufus (= *rosso,* 'reddish,' Carratello {1992, 193-94})."

"Certainly" is a strong word in relation to truth or falsity regarding the people and events of more than two millennia ago, especially with respect to a song-poem written with tongue-in-cheek about a front door that can hear whisperings from inside 'her' house, and verbally relate them to a passing stranger.[95]

Green provides no further explanation of why he summarily excludes Caelius Rufus as the referent of Catullus's description (67:46-47) of a man who is *longus* <tall>, as is Caelius Rufus;[96] has *rubra* <reddish> hair, as is likely of a man with the nickname *Rufus* <"Rusty">; has an intimidating temper, *ne ... supersilia tollet* <lest he *arch* his eyebrows>, as does Caelius Rufus,[97] and has been involved in *magnas ... lites*

<great arguments, thus legal arguments, and thus litigation>, as has Caelius Rufus (*see* pp. 22-35 above).

If the manuscripts are at all reflective of what Catullus actually has written in these two verses, he surely realizes that future readers would know that this description fits the *Caelius Rufus* they would recognize from *Pro Caelio*.

Interestingly, it appears that Green is not unaware (Carratello's article notwithstanding) that the only way Catullus (or his hypothetical posthumous editor) could have hoped that future readers would 'get' this lampoon is if the tall, intimidating, russet-browed litigant is, indeed, Caelius Rufus. Thus, with a 'wink', Green describes him as "the **rufous** stranger" [emphasis added]. As is obvious from his 2005 Latin text-plus-translation, *The Poems of Catullus: A Bilingual Edition*, Green is a superb wordsmith. It is not mere coincidence that he uses here the relatively obscure cognate "rufous", both a homonym for "Rufus" and a synonym for reddish.

Seeing Is Not *Believing*

In the article Green cites, Carratello (pp. 193-94) addresses the issue thus:

> *Chi sia il* longus homo *vorrebbe giustamente sapere R. Verdière, che si domanda se le sue rosse sopracciglia non autorizzino a vedere in lui il Rosso, il* Rufus *o il* Caelius Rufus, *dei quali si trova il ricordo in Catullo. Un* Rufus *compare nel c. 69: è un uomo col quale non vogliono andare a letto le ragazze per le sue ascelle puzzolenti ... [ellipsis sic] Nel c. 77 Rufo è presentato come l'amico del quale il poeta s'è vanamente fidato, perché il falso amico gli ha sottratto la sua Lesbia: si tratta di Celio Rufo. È probabile che di lui si parli anche nei cc. 69 e 71 (nel 71 non è fatto il nome, ma facilmente si intuisce, di colui al quale puzzano terribilmente le ascelle). Sicuramente Celio Rufo è il Celio del carme 58 (Caeli, Lesbia nostra ... [ellipsis sic] / glubit magnanimi Remi nepotes), ben distinto dal Celio veronese del 100, l'innamorato di Aufilleno: niente, infatti, collega Celio Rufo con Verona. Che il* Rufulus *di 59, 1 (Bononiensis Rufa Rufulum fellat) possa essere il* Rufus *dei cc. 69 e 77 non c'è ragione di supporlo; allo stesso modo manca ogni appiglio per identificare* Rufus (Caelius Rufus) *con il*

longus homo *di 67, 45-48, per noi destinato a rimanere un ignoto.*

R. Verdière justifiably wants to know: Who is the *longus homo* [<tall man>]? He asks: Would not the red eyebrows permit seeing him as "[Caelius] the Red", "[Caelius] the Rufous", *ie*, the Caelius Rufus who is found elsewhere in the Catullan record?

For comparison, a Rufus is in Poem 69: a man with whom the gals do not want to go to bed because his armpits stink. In Poem 77, Rufus is presented as the friend of the poet he himself trusted in vain, because the false friend has stolen his Lesbia: a deed of Caelius Rufus himself.

It is likely that [Catullus] speaks of him in Poems 69 and 71 too. (In 71, the name is not given, but he whose armpits stink terribly is easily guessed.)

Assuredly, Caelius Rufus is the Caelius of song-poem 58 (*Caeli, Lesbia nostra ... / glubit magnanimi Remi nepotes* [<Caelius, *Our* Lesbia ... peels back the magnificent Sons of Remus>]), quite distinct from the Veronese Caelius of Poem 100, the *inamorato* of Aufillenus: Nothing, in fact, connects Caelius Rufus with Verona.

There is no basis to suppose that the *Rufulus* [<Little Rufie>] of Poem 59:1 (*bononiensis rufa rufulum fellat* [<Rufa of Bologna fellates Little Rufie>]) could be the Rufus of Poems 69 and 77. In the same way, to identify Rufus (*ie*, Caelius Rufus) with the *homo longus* of Poem 67:45-48 lacks any grounding. For us, it is destined to remain an unknown.

Carratello is an eminent scholar, by any measure.[98] Yet, though scholars are trained to carefully sift evidence and draw from it rational conclusions, here he displays an intellectual inflexibility sometimes found in critics (and all of us): Presenting evidence, staring it in the face, and then positing that it either supports an inference opposite to that which it obviously does support, or that the evidence they are staring at does not exist at all.[99]

Carratello has referenced Carmen 100:1-2 <u>xrl.us/bmfbyy</u>, the clear implication of which is that Caelius Rufus has spent at least *some* portion of his youth in Verona (*Caelius.../flos Veronensum ... iuvenum* <Caelius.../ flower of Veronese youth>) ... and then Carratello writes at once: *niente, infatti, collega Celio Rufo con Verona* <Nothing, in fact, connects Caelius Rufus with Verona>!

As indicated above (pp. 47-48), that Caelius's family is (possibly[100]) based in Teramo presents no barrier to Caelius having some boyhood connection to Verona. Abraham Lincoln, not without cause, is claimed by three US states: Kentucky, Indiana, and Illinois. Barack Obama is claimed by Hawaii and Illinois – and even Jakarta, Indonesia.[101]

In the wake of Catiline's failed conspiracy against the Roman Republic, Caelius spends two years in Africa tending to his family's business interests there (Wiseman 1987, p. 64). Since his family has such substantial interests in Africa, it is not implausible that it has business interests (as well as extended family) closer to home, in thriving Verona, where Caelius may have summered during some period of his youth.

No Poem Is an Island

Quinn observes (1972a, p. xi):

> [A poem] is not absolutely autonomous: it needs a response to come fully into existence. It may also require knowledge on our part, as well as our willingness and our ability to respond. Our response, in other words, is controlled – not only by the verbal structure, but what the poet feels he can rely on every reader to know .... [A]dequate understanding of it will depend often on acquaintance with other poems by the same poet; the more a poet's *oeuvre* hangs together, the more the poet's other poems are present in each of them – they represent, if we like to think of it that way, a special instance of the things the poet relies on us to know.

As set forth above, it is known that Caelius Rufus is tall, temperamental, and has been involved in well-known litigation. His red hair is readily inferred from his nickname, "Rusty". Catullus signals that *Pro Caelio* is part of his trove of allusion in *Carmen* 49, which profusely thanks Cicero – without speci-fying *what* he is thanking Cicero for. The only explanation I find plausible for this lacuna is that Catullus cannot *expli-citly* salute Cicero for his success in *Pro Caelio* without losing the little game Catullus plays with listeners/readers: *preten-ding* that he has not revealed Clodia as *Lesbia*. As Wiseman himself astutely observes of Catullus's use of pseudonyms generally (1987, p. 133): **"The pretense of concealment is just part of the joke."** [Emphasis added.]

Catullus virtually draws a picture of Caelius Rufus in the fi-nal verses of *Carmen* 67. Other than spelling-out the joke to listeners/readers, it is hard to imagine what Catullus can do to make it more clear that the slave-girl gossip that he has shrewdly versified through the device of a talkative Door con-cerns Clodia, Caelius, and the argument that has led to their sensational confrontation in *Pro Caelio*.

A Counsel of Surrender

In annotations, Carratello (p. 194, n. 7 and 8) characterizes as *stravagante* <ridiculous> István Károly Horvàth's sugges-tion that the mystery man is Catullus. For good measure, Car-ratello dismisses Colin W Macleod's conjecture that he is the *Caecilius* of 67:9 as *né meno assurda* <no less absurd>.

Though I disagree with their respective solutions, at least Horvàth and Macleod – and Skinner – have advanced them. To assert *per noi destinato a rimanere un ignoto* <for us, it is destined to remain an unknown> is a counsel of *surrender* (cf. p. 89 below).

Forbidden Fruit

For some scholars, to identify the unnamed man of 67:45-48 as *Caelius* would require backtracking from, or at least sub-stantially modifying, stances they have taken on broader is-sues. Of some such stances, Quinn comments (1972b, p. 138): "It is good scholarly method to explore them. The trouble is that those who explore them become attached to them."

Copley (1957, p. v), in the thrall of the New Criticism xrl.us/b mejzj (then at the height of its influence), must restrict his reading to the four corners of the text: "A lyric poem is itself.

It tells us all that we need to know about itself, or at least all that the poet wanted us to know about it .... No one lyric poem depends on any other for its worth or meaning; it is itself, a whole, an entity, a complete unit of thought." Thus, Copley cannot refer to Catullus's other works, much less to Cicero's *Pro Caelio*, in his interpretation of *Carmen* 67.

Copley thereby spares his students, as well as general readers, agonies (such as the present exercise) as a precondition for understanding *Carmen* 67. But, in ruling out information external to the song-poem itself, he also rules out the possibility that those same students and general readers will ever discover the real targets of what he himself describes as "a *diffamatio*, a lampoon; its purpose is to defame and ridicule."

Wiseman, like a moth fascinated by a flame, comes ever so close to realizing (or admitting) that *Carmen* 67 is about Clodia *Metelli*. In a chapter entitled "Lesbia Illa" <*That* Lesbia> (58:1), he discusses the use of pseudonyms by Roman authors of this period generally, and by Catullus particularly. Wiseman writes of *Carmen* 67 (1987, pp. 130, 133):

> Even in the permissive climate of the fifties B.C., a formal anonymity was required to protect the reputation of a person of quality ..... [But,] it was not through fear of consequences that Catullus refused to name the litigious adulterer with the ginger eyebrows .... **He was teasing his audience, inviting them to guess the name** ... [Emphasis added.]

Wiseman (1987, pp. 127-28), notably, directs a spotlight at the performative dimension of Catullus's song-poems:[102]

> [I]f Virgil could read three books of the *Aeneid* to Augustus and Octavia, presumably Catullus could read the *Peleus and Thetis* [*Carmen* 64 xrl.us/bmfcdp] to his privileged friends. An alternative possibility, however, is suggested by poem 67, the dialogue with the door. Where two voices are needed to read the poem effectively, we are moving from recitation proper to dramatic performance – if indeed any such clear distinction was ever made in the ancient world.

Further, Wiseman (1969, p. 36) realizes:

Lesbia herself was certainly not unknown to the *provincia* [Verona] ... poem 86 [xrl.us/bmfcgd] compares her with a Quintia who was certainly Veronese, and Quintia's brother evidently was paying some attention to her. Their fellow-townsman Caelius was a true friend[?] to Catullus "cum vesana meas torreret flamma medullas" [<when mad fire roared in my guts> *Carmen* 100:7] – surely a reference to his affair with Lesbia.

Yet, as noted above, Wiseman (1996, p. 56) writes: "Catullus' Caelius was Veronese; M. Caelius Rufus came from [Teramo]", as if two different locales are logically excluded for *Caelius Rufus* – but not for *Lesbia*.

Wiseman concedes that one of the three sisters is Lesbia (*see* this page, below). As members of the *gens* Claudii, no one is more Roman than they. But (at least) one of them "was certainly not unknown to" Verona. Why then would Caelius Rufus, even if essentially Teramese, be any less likely than Clodia to be known in Verona?

A big-picture thinker such as Wiseman would surely be aware that though contemporaneous audiences, familiar with much of the minutia of that time, might be able "to guess the name" of some relatively obscure "litigious adulterer with the ginger eyebrows", nonetheless Catullus would know that, for *future* audiences/readers, that thumbnail description would conjure the name of only one individual: *Caelius Rufus*.

However, Wiseman cannot 'go there'. He is perhaps most often cited by other commentators for his skepticism that the Lesbia of Catullus's poetry is the Clodia Metelli of Cicero's prose (1987, pp. 2, 136; *see* also Appendices D and F below):

> ... "Lesbia" herself is commonly identified with Clodia Metelli rather than either of her sisters (despite the chronological problems involved) because her notoriety is more conspicuous for us than that of Clodia [*sic; see* Appendix D] Luculli; but if, instead of Cicero's speech in defence of Caelius, we happened to possess the text of L. Lentulus' speech prosecuting Clodius in 61 B.C. [*see* pp. 12-17 above], precisely the reverse would be the case.

..... [Lesbia] was a noblewoman, from the same family as Clodia Metelli ... conceivably even Clodia Metelli herself, more probably one of her sisters.

Hence, if Wiseman reads the "litigious adulterer with the ginger eyebrows" as Caelius Rufus, then he must admit that Catullus's Lesbia can be *only* Cicero's Clodia Metelli. Having conceded that Lesbia *might be* Clodia Metelli, and having brought up the "litigious adulterer" of *Carmen* 67 only a few pages into a chapter entitled "Lesbia Illa", Wiseman stops short, *ex silencio*, of allowing his best known hypothesis to go up in flames.

Skinner is similarly constrained by her overall thesis regarding Clodia Metelli – not as to Clodia Metelli's identification as Lesbia (which Skinner accepts as more likely than not), but as to Clodia's character, which Skinner asserts to be approximately that of, say, Jacqueline Kennedy Onassis.[103]

In her PhD dissertation of 1975-6 (published as a monograph in 1981), Skinner presents her overview (1981, p. vi):

[S]everal critics .... argue that generations of commentators have been fooled by a carefully contrived illusion of sincerity. The autobiographical element in Catullus' poems is actually an artistic device employed to color a generic situation; although real names and real events project an impression of verisimilitude, the pieces are ingenious fictions. To interpret them by constructing "factual" circumstances of composition which will explain their obscurities and anomalies is as futile as speculating on the names of Lady Macbeth's children.

Traditionalist scholars are hereby warned that this study firmly adheres to the new approach outlined above. The poems are viewed as constructs of the imagination not personal but artistic and dramatic truths.

(However, Shakespeare does not purport to be having an ongoing affair with any of Lady Macbeth's offspring. It would surely be interesting, though, to know if the "Dark Lady" of the wedded Shakespeare's sonnets were based upon a real-life model, and if so, biographical details about that model.)

Skinner (1983, p. 287) succinctly summarizes her position thus: "[T]he Clodia of history turns out to be the direct antithesis of the Clodia of myth."

As recently as 2010 (p. 7), Skinner writes:

> [Was Clodia's] actual conduct, as far as we can determine it, deviant? Conspicuous though she was, there is, as we shall see, no trustworthy evidence that she violated behavioral norms for women of her rank, marital status, and age. Only in her publicly censured relationship with her youngest brother was she at all singular.[104]

Heir Non-Apparent

Green (2005, p. 250), acknowledging Kroll and Skinner, extracts from the morass of scholarly esoterica the crux of *Carmen* 67: "[W]hat lurks behind the whole scenario (Skinner 2003, 48-49) is a *lack of heirs* ... " [Emphasis in original.]

In Skinner's words (2003, p. 48):

> [B]etween the later 70s and 66 B.C.E., a change in the praetorian edict, specifically the introduction of the clause *unde cognati* [<from which relations>], allowed blood relatives of the deceased on either side to supersede members of the wider *gens* [<extended family>] as claimants to the estate in cases of intestacy (Gardner 25-34).

On the same page and the one that follows, Skinner writes of *Carmen* 67's mystery paramour:

> Unlike the intrigues with Postumius and Cornelius, this relationship was apparently of longer duration (*addebat*, 45) [per Skinner: <she kept mentioning>]. Furthermore, the anonymous individual is, presumably, in a good position to learn of the Door's talebearing as well as **a particularly hotheaded type** .....

> As for the **tall man** ..... **a subsequent lawsuit** depends for its climactic effect upon positive revelation of the **auburn-haired** man's identity. The Door's report of the fellow's physical appearance is, as Macleod notes, a rhetorical strategy for proclaiming it indirectly. He rightly perceives that the economy of satire demands the impli-

cation of someone already involved in the poem's action, **not an unknown outsider**. [Emphasis added.]

In other words: the Marcus Caelius Rufus of *Pro Caelio*.

But, that identification would be an embarrassment to the proposition that Clodia's intimacy with her *brother* was her *only* "deviant" relationship.

Skinner (p. 49) further notes:

> Accordingly, Macleod proposes the Caecilius who is now the Door's master, on the grounds that he is "[t]he only person whom poem 67 offers us to attach to the description of lines 45-8."

(Note, though, that Macleod's suggestion is implicitly contradicted by the Door {67:45-46}: *quem dicere nolo / nomine ne tollat rubra supercilia* <whose name / I don't want to say, lest he *arch* russet eyebrows>.)

Skinner continues:

> But that is obviously a counsel of desperation, for we have not been previously informed that Caecilius, or any other character mentioned in the text, was tall and auburn-haired.

However, Catullus's readers/listeners have indeed been informed of such a character by Cicero, relatively recently, because it is likely that Catullus dies about two years after the trial of Caelius, and hence his readers/listeners surely remember it while Catullus still lives.

Further, Caelius himself is on the scene at that point, as are Clodia and her newest *poetae tenero* (35:1): Caecilius II.

Whether or not aware of Horvàth's suggestion or Carratello's dismissive comment regarding it, Skinner (p. 49) presents a clever (and brave) solution to *Carmen* 67: The *poet* did it!:

> It is more reasonable to suppose, instead, that a listening audience was being invited to use its own eyes. If the poem was orally performed at Rome, the "sting in the tail" would consist in the Door – who has ears and a tongue, as we are told (44), but not organs of vision – giving, un-

beknownst to her, a good description of the performer Catullus.

Yet, Catullus could not have expected *future* readers to know that he fits this visual description, as it is mentioned nowhere in his body of work – or anyone else's.

Skinner continues further (pp. 48-49):

> [T]he entire story being bruited about is at best hearsay, at worst gossip resting upon shaky foundations. The equivocal, sometimes contradictory, nature of the account points in the same direction: that Catullus' listeners might not agree upon the basic facts of the case after hearing the poem recited – **especially if they tried to pick it apart as scholars do nowadays** – could be a calculated part of the joke. Thus the conclusion would be appropriately ironic only if the nosy inquirer were to hear himself maligned by what he and his audience knew to be a grossly false accusation ... [Emphasis added.]

The premise is on point, *ie*, that this is an example of what a modern-day journalist might impishly call "a story too good to check". The individual reader/listener is implicitly invited to believe all of it, parts of it, or none of it, at her or his option. As such, it undercuts Giangrande's apparent view (*see* pp. 93-104 below) that *Carmen* 67 can be subjected to rigorous logical analysis that will yield one, and only one, perfectly consistent narrative (even though the accuracy of the manuscript itself is problematic) – in a lampoon that employs many instances of weasel words such as "they *say*".[105]

But, I do not find that the Door's equivocal and sometimes contradictory gossip requires that *Carmen* 67 end on a note of irony. Nor do I find, if Catullus were the Door's (inadvertent) target, that "he and his audience knew to be a grossly false accusation" that Catullus has had an affair with a married woman. On the contrary, what Catullus is *most known* for is having an affair with a married woman: Clodia.

Moreover, Catullus is further known as one of the leading New Poets. Their characteristic subject matter is the stuff of daily life (rather than, say, heroic epics). A sparrow shall not fall on the ground, nor shall a napkin be purloined from his dinner table, without Catullus versifying the event.[106] If Catullus were in a great lawsuit, I believe he would write a song-poem of its own about it, and that that song-poem would be included in the surviving collection.

Further still, if Catullus has the Door merely confabulating events that have not occurred in order for Catullus to embarrass himself as the Interlocutor the Door cannot see, *Carmen* 67 loses much of its punch as *paraclausithyron* turned *diffamatio*. Hence, reading Catullus as the unnamed paramour /litigator contradicts both the general understanding of the program of the New Poets, and the inescapable sense of *Carmen* 67 as an actual, rather than *faux, diffamatio*.

Acknowledging Macleod and William Fitzgerald, Skinner explores in the same passage (pp. 49-50) *Carmen* 67's debt to Callimachus:

> In its original setting as part of the composer's repertoire, then, poem 67 could be perceived as among other things a broad parody of the investigations elegantly carried out in [Callimachus's] *Aetia* <Origins> [xrl.us/bk7krj]. Activities in a distant town are the object of inquiry, but gossip takes the place of pedantry. Allusion to a recent modification in the inheritance laws interjects topical commentary: the change would have affected a good many families and attempts to circumvent it may have caused the same kind of outrage as the cynical practice of courting the rich and childless in hopes of a bequest (cf. Hor. S. 2.5 [xrl.us/bk7kqc]). Finally, the insertion of self-betraying *biographèmes* involving place of origin and physical appearance undermines the aetiologist's academic stance by embroiling him personally in the reported action. Nevertheless, the elegy is fundamentally good-humored[?] As in poem 10, the entertainer Catullus, a well-known figure on the Roman social scene, makes fun of his own public image through an embarrassing encounter: here his stance as literary personality and leading proponent of a Callimachean aesthetic is deftly skewered.[107]

I hope it is not too impertinent to suggest that pedantry has retaken gossip. This reader's understanding is certainly enriched by learning that Paul Murgatroyd's observation that

Carmen 67's canny parodying of a Callimachean *paraclau-sithyron* can be expanded to include Catullus's likewise parodying of Callimachus's *Aetia*.

Yet note: Copley (1953, p. 149) begins an article on *Carmen* 35:

> The cumulative commentary on this poem, although massively learned and very informative, leaves the reader with a sense of disappointment; he feels that he has learned much, but that he still does not know what the poem means, what its author's purposes and intentions were, and what he wished his readers to know and feel. For the commentaries leave unanswered, or answer in a hesitating and uncertain way, the questions that are really crucial...

That *Carmen* 67 parodies Callimachus's *Aetia* exemplifies Catullus's genius for crafting that which is patently vulgar into that which is *lepidus* <swank, but suave>. But this insight, standing by itself, does not confront the issue that even if the unnamed paramour is *incorrectly* rumored to be Catullus, how, then, could the wife not be rumored, even if incorrectly, to be Clodia; her husband, then, not be Celer; and the tall russet-browed man involved in a messy lawsuit, therefore, not be *Caelius?* In Copley's words: "the questions that are really crucial".

Regarding "self-betraying *biographèmes* involving place of origin and physical appearance", that the Door and the Interlocutor are, apparently, both from Verona does little to narrow the list of suspects to Catullus, and as noted, the physical appearance, so far as surviving documents indicate, is that of Caelius, not Catullus.

I am in accord with the broader point of Copley's sentiment (1953, p. 152) regarding *Carmen* 35, as quoted at the beginning of this work:

> [I]f my meaning is different from, or even contradictory to, yours, have we done anything but demonstrate the essential richness of the poem in question? Certainly a plurality of meanings is better than no meaning at all.

To be sure, Catullus is a poet, not a copyist in the census-taker's office.

But, though *Carmen* 10 <u>xrl.us/bmfn</u> is certainly self-depre-catory, on the other hand Catullus there plays no coy games about identifying himself and the other *dramatis personae:* Varus and Cinna. Varus's *inamorata*-of-the-nonce need not be named, because she is merely the cypher required to unmask Catullus's *ad hoc* pretension to have returned from public service in Bithynia not *completely* empty-handed. No maddeningly confusing details; no riddle; no enigma.

Carmen 67, unlike *Carmen* 10, rather than building up to the Interlocutor's embarrassment, instead revolves around guessing the identity of the adulterous wife, her inadequate husband, and his lusty father – in addition to that of the tall, temperamental russet-browed litigant.

Catullus himself may not believe *all* of the rumors about the Door's household. But, he is surely not discouraging his listeners/readers from believing any or all of them at their option, so there is no internal logic for Catullus making himself the subject of a false rumor.

In the last analysis, if the tall russet-browed man involved in a great lawsuit is a reference to Caelius, then at once the other unnamed (or ambiguously named) main characters are known: Clodia, Celer, and Celer's father, Baldy. Only if he is anyone other than Caelius is Carratello's pessimism then warranted: We are destined to never know.

Giangrande's Exegesis

Skinner's reading of *Carmen* 67 presents a solution to the mystery of the russet-browed man, and an intelligent defense thereof. In doing so, she covers well the scholarly commentary since 1980.

For useful summaries of the century of commentary on *Carmen* 67 prior to 1970, Giangrande provides 48 pages inter-mixed with 126 footnotes (in the main pointedly disagreeing with the interpretations of other scholars). Yet his own solution, not presented in-whole until the final three pages, not only fails to identify any of the song-poem's characters, it also moves the Door from Verona to Brescia, making incoherent the Door's defense – against her rumored dereliction in ensuring the marital fidelity of the lady of the house – that the lady had 'a past' in Brescia *before* ever arriving as a bride under the Door's watch. (His 'workaround' is quite resourceful, as shall be seen.)

Giangrande is commendable, though, for providing a rundown of every 'family' (*eg*, number of husbands, number of houses, number of locales) of erroneous interpretations (including his own) that emerge during the century leading up to his article's publication. He is also very good about spelling out the text as contained in the surviving manuscripts, as well as the noteworthy emendations that scholars have made since the Renaissance.

Giangrande (p. 115) posits, without reservation, an emendation of his own: *Veronae* → *matronae* (67:34), thereby eliminating any mention of Verona in the song-poem, and thus allowing (indeed, requiring) the Door to be located in Brescia. Since there is likely (though not *necessarily*, given the fluid nature of performative art) only one correct text, but many possibilities for erroneous speculation, the odds are not in favor of an emendation being correct at this late date. Interestingly, though, Giangrande's forcefully fought-for emendation results in a citation by Thomson to an article by Giuseppe Billanovich that purports to provide a glimpse into how leisure time is spent by two particular monks in a medieval monastery in Brescia (*see* pp. 104-07 below).

In Giangrande's words (p. 85), with which I concur:

> [T]he only way to solve the problem will be to submit both the poem itself and the arguments brought forward by the critics to the most exhaustive logical analysis possible, leaving no detail unexamined.

To this end, Giangrande proceeds to unpack *Carmen* 67 in linear fashion, leaving no important prior controversy ignored or evaded. Thus, though a reader might (in all likelihood will) disagree with Giangrande on one point or another, by studying Giangrande's article in some detail the reader will become versed in almost all of the major issues raised by earlier critics about this song-poem.

Carmen 67 begins with an unnamed Interlocutor offering a standard greeting to a Roman matron:

> *o dulci iucunda viro iucunda parenti*
> *salve teque bona iuppiter auctet ope* (1-2)

> Oh joy to a sweet husband, joy to a father – *salutations*
> And, may goodness redound to you by God's grace

In light of the rumors of cuckoldry that follow, *dulci* <sweet> has in Latin the same duality as in English: The difference between a man being called "sweet" by, for example, his wife, versus when deemed so by another man.

> *ianua quam balbo dicunt servisse benigne*
> *olim cum sedes ipse senex tenuit* (3-4)

> Miss Door, whom they say to have slaved *benignly*
> for *Baldy* (earlier – when Senior *himself* held the seat of
>   power)

The first surprise is that the Interlocutor is addressing a *door* – and by implication a slave-girl – not a *matron*, as the greeting would lead an ancient listener/reader to expect. Thus, the tongue-in-cheek mood is set.

Second, the alert listener/reader would recall that *Balbo* <Baldy> is also the nickname of the third prosecution speaker in *Pro Caelio*, Lucius Herennius Balbus.[108] Hence, the song-poem's subtext is hinted at. Surely, *ipse senex* <Senior himself> (67:4) is the *Balbo* of 67:3, as well as the *parenti* <father> of 67:1.

In order to elicit the Door's version of events, the Interlocutor teasingly points out to 'her' that she has been rumored to have succeeded in keeping the lady of the house faithful (to *Baldy*) while Baldy was alive, but has failed to do so on behalf of Baldy's son, who has become her husband:

> *quamque ferunt rursus voto servisse maligne*
> *postquam est porrecto facta marita sene*
> *dic agedum nobis quare mutata feraris*
> *in dominum veterem deseruisse fidem* (5-8)

yet whom (they rumor), reneging on responsibility,
ever since Senior was laid to rest served *malignly*
    the vow made in marriage.
Tell us *why* you would be rumored to have changed
    course
from having slaved so faithfully for the Old Master?

My reading agrees with Giangrande (p. 86) to the extent that there is no need to change *voto* <vow> to *nato* (or *gnato*) <son>, nor (*contra* Aldine) *est* to *es*, nor (*contra* Ernst Badian, p. 88 ff.) *facta* to *pacta* (ie, in my reading, the *marriage vow* has been made, thus avoiding the *Door* having nuptials).

The Door replies:

> *non ita caecilio placeam cui tradita nunc sum*
> *culpa mea est quamquam dicitur esse mea*
> *nec peccatum a me quisquam pote dicere quicquam* (9-11)

No fault is *mine!* Although, it is *said* to be mine.
(I must now likewise please *Caecilius,*
    having been conveyed to *him.*)
Nor can anyone accuse me of any *wrong!*

Here Catullus caricatures a slave's pleas of innocence, consistent with the stereotypes of the Roman comic stage of the time (as Clodia may have done in one of more of her plays).[109] But he also provides a further clue as to the identity of his targets: *ita caecilio placeam cui tradita nunc sum* <(I must now likewise please *Caecilius,*[110] having been conveyed to *him*)>.

Giangrande, seeking to avoid a third male occupant of the House of Balbus, apparently fails to realize that verse 9 is a *parenthetic* remark, though every other translation I have read (not a few) recognizes it as such by surrounding it either in parentheses or em dashes, and though its interposition between *non* <No...> and *sum culpa mea est* <... fault is *mine!*> makes this clause plainly parenthetic.

Giangrande does realize that *Caecilius* is a reference, in part, to Balbus's son. But this fact, by itself, does not account for Catullus interjecting news of a property conveyance mid-sentence within the Door's general plaint of innocence of dereliction. If, as Giangrande believes, there were no 'third man' in addition to Balbus and son, the conveyance of the house from father to son would be assumed. The significance of this interjection can only be that the son, like his father, no longer occupies the house – and another man does (*ie*, the Caecilius II of *Carmen* 35).

Were Giangrande to note, as does Thomson (*see* n. 110 below), that *Caecilius* in 67:9 refers also to the *Caecilius* of 35:1, and were both to recognize that the *sapphica puella* / *musa doctior* <Sapphic Mistress more knowing than a Muse> of 35:16-17, in the context of Catullus's *oeuvre*, can *only* be Clodia, then they would realize that *Caecilius* is a double-*entendre* referring to both Clodia's husband, Quintus Caecilius Metellus Celer (Caecilius I), and the new *Caecilius* in Clodia's life (Caecilius II). The latter has poetic pretensions that Catullus mocks in 35:1 (*poetae tenero* <touching poet>), and skewers here in 67:32-34, as shall be seen. In other words, there is only one husband and only one marital home – but there are two *Caecilii*.

The Door continues to complain about the injustice in her life:

> *verum istius populi ianua qui te facit*
> *qui quacumque aliquid reperitur non bene factum*
> *ad me omnes clamant ianua culpa tua est*   (12-14)

To be sure, the *townspeople:* "The *Door* did it!"
When anything *whatsoever* is discovered to have not
    gone well,
they *all* shout at *me*, "It's *your* fault, Door!"

There is more here than an ancillary's routine complaint (which too often is justified) about being wrongfully blamed. Implicit in her complaint is that 1) at times, she is aware of what *townspeople* are saying, and 2) the rumored conduct is the *culpa* <fault> of someone *other* than herself.

The Interlocutor eggs-on the Door:

> *non istuc satis est uno te dicere verbo*
> *sed facere ut quivis sentiat et videat*   (15-16)

Saying a word is not enough;
instead, make it so that anyone[111] can *see* and *feel*.

The Door, claiming helplessness, replies with another of her grievances – being ignored:

> *qui possum nemo quaerit nec scire laborat* (17)

How *can* I? No one *asks* – or *wants* to find out.

The Interlocutor humors her, by pointing out the obvious:

> *nos volumus nobis dicere ne dubita* (18)

Indubitably, *we* do! Tell us!

Having restrained herself as long as she could, with just a bit of coaxing by the Interlocutor the Door now gushes forth with gossip to the effect that the lady of the house is no 'lady' at the time of her marriage; that her husband's male member is inadequate in size, functionality, and procreative capability; and that his father, while alive, is her intimate partner in the son's stead:

> *primum igitur virgo quod fertur tradita nobis*
> *falsum est non illam vir prior attigerit*
> *languidior tenera cui pendens sicula beta*
> *numquam se mediam sustulit ad tunicam*
>
> *sed pater illius gnati violasse cubile*
> *dicitur et miseram conscelerasse domum*
> *sive quod impia mens caeco flagrabat amore*
> *seu quod iners sterili semine natus erat*
> *et quaerendus is unde foret nervosius illud*
> *quod posset zonam solvere virgineam* (19-28)

Well then ... *first* of all: The 'virgin' brought us
    was a *fraudulent conveyance!*[112]
(Not that the groom *could have* touched her beforehand,
he who, *little* dagger drooping limper than the letter
    lambda,[113]
never got it up to half-mast!)
But, the *father* is said to have violated the son's marriage
    bed,
and to have defiled the disgraced[114] domicile –
whether because *his* filthy mind was ablaze with blind
    lust,
or because the impotent son's semen was sterile,

and *she* sought from whatever source that stronger
   muscle
that could untie a virgin's *not*.[115]

Critics have generated much confusion over the meaning of
prior in 67:21. There are those who read *prior* as "previous",
an adjective modifying the subject, *vir*, thus (Green 2005,
p.167): *non illam vir prior attigerit* = "she'd not been touched /
by her previous husband". On the other hand, there are
critics who read *prior* as an adverb, *eg*, "previous*ly*", and thus
<not that the groom *could have* touched her *beforehand*>.[116]

Of the two-husband reading that "her previous husband" would
imply, Macleod (p. 188) observes:

> [It] introduces a pointless complication and takes all the
> sting out of *virgo quod fertur tradita nobis falsum est* [<the
> 'virgin' brought us was a *fraudulent conveyance!*>] (19-20);
> if the woman had been married before, no one would ever
> have supposed she was a virgin when she married
> Balbus [*sic*].

Giangrande (pp. 102-03) provides an example of the tangled
web some scholars have woven in order to rationalize the two-
husband reading:

> Friedrich argues as follows: since it is a priori "unmö-
> glich" [<impossible>] (sic) ["(sic)" per Giangrande] that the
> marriage could be celebrated immediately after the death
> of Balbus (he thinks that Balbus was the lady's father,
> and that the impossibility is dictated by reasons of eti-
> quette: one should not marry during the mourning peri-
> od), the girl must therefore have been married before en-
> tering Balbus' house, upon his death; she is, however,
> said to have been *tradita* [<conveyed>] to the door of Bal-
> bus' house still as a virgin. How is this possible? She
> must have at first moved from Balbus' house, as a *nova
> nupta* [<newlywed>], into her first husband's house; her
> first husband did not deflower her, because he was impo-
> tent, but she consoled herself with his father and others
> (Postumius, Cornelius) and continued to live with him
> until her father died; upon her father's death her first
> husband sold his house, and the couple moved into Bal-

bus' house, which the woman had inherited and now re-entered as a *marita* [<wife>]. Finally, the woman divorced her *vir prior* [<prior husband>], on grounds of his impotence, claiming to still be a virgin.

This is far from Copley's standard for a *diffamatio*, which "by its very nature, has to have a simple solution", or Skinner's description (2003, p. 50) of song-poem 67 as "what must have been originally a breezy performance piece".

Catullus now interjects comic relief by having the Interlocutor remark sarcastically:

> *egregium narras mira pietate parentem*
> *qui ipse sui gnati minxerit in gremium* (29-30)

> You tell a tale about an *excellent* parent of *admirable*
>   piety –
> who would *squirt*[117] in his own son's *lap!*

There follows another passage that has given rise to much controversy, some I think not very important; some, quite so:

> *atqui non solum hoc se dicit cognitum habere*
> *brixia chinea suppositum specula*
> *flavus quam molli praecurrit flumine mella*
> *brixia veronae mater amata meae*
> *sed de postumio et corneli narrat amore*
> *cum quibus illa malum fecit adulterium* (31-36)

> And not only is *he himself* said to have had
>   this carnal knowledge.
> *Brescia*, set 'neath China Hill[118] look-out,
> where the yellow Mello river gently flows;
> *Brescia*, beloved mother of *Verona mia* –
> *even it* tells tales of amours with Postumius and
>   Cornelius;
> with whom *both*, she committed the sin of *adultery!*

One disagreement regards whether *chinea* in the manuscript should be replaced by *cycneae* <swan>; another as to whether the river Mello (or *Mella*) *praecurrit* <runs *before*> or *percurrit* <runs *through*> the ancient boundaries of Brescia.

Neither controversy brings this reader any closer to understanding what, or whom, this song-poem is about.

The word *adulterium* <adultery>, itself, is not contested. But,
it is cited by some as support for the two-husband reading
because, as a legal technicality, adultery requires the female
partner to be married to someone – other than her paramour.
Thus, the two-husband reading typically runs, the woman
cuckolded both the prior husband while in Brescia, to the
benefit of Postumius and Cornelius; and she cuckolded a second husband after arriving as a bride at the house the Door
watches-over in Verona. Giangrande's above quotation of Frie-
drich shows the complications the two-husband reading requires to avoid internal contradiction.

However, Catullus has cast the Door neither as a cartologist
for Brescia and its environs, nor as a word-parsing matrimo-
nial lawyer, but rather as an excitable, indignant, and gossipy slave-girl. Then as now – particularly in the mind of someone excitable, indignant, and gossipy – adultery runs the gamut
of affairs out of wedlock.[119]

"Mental Error"

Of more relevance – to the issue of the who and the what – is
the line *brixia veronae mater amata meae* <Brescia, beloved
mother of *Verona mia* >. (A modern analogy might be "Brook-
lyn, beloved mother of *my Manhattan*"[?!])

Giangrande pointedly asks (p. 107):

> Why should the door i.e. Catullus, bother to emphasize
> that Brixia [<Brescia>] was the metropolis of Verona? The
> point is totally irrelevant to the context; indeed it is inop-
> portune. Why should he want to gratuitously antagonize
> his readers by reminding them that Brixia was more im-
> portant than their town?

Especially so since neither then nor now is Brescia in any sense
more important than Verona. Giangrande (p. 112) asks, rhetorically, "Could it be that we have one town too many, just as ...
the critics had postulated one husband too many?" (But note:
unlike a 2nd husband, Verona and Brixia are explicitly in the
text.)

Wiseman (1987, p. 110) suggests: "The new colonies equipped themselves with a legendary past – hence 'Brixia, mother of my Verona' ... " But, why legendary descent from *Brescia* – which is hardly as romantic a legend as, say, Rome's descent from Troy? And, even if this *were* a Veronese legend, why would *the Door*, personified as a *Veronese* slave-girl, suddenly be waxing poetic about *Brescia's* legendary importance? In Giangrande's words (p. 112): "[T]he town is in any case described with an enthusiasm that has puzzled scholars because apparently irrelevant to the context ..."

Moreover, the Door is *suffixa tigillo* <affixed to the lintel>. Giangrande (p. 113) asks: "[H]ow could it possibly be versed in local antiquarian lore, and know that Brixia was the metropolis of Verona?"[120]

Giangrande resourcefully resolves this element of the riddle by eliminating *Veronae* from the text and inserting in its stead *matronae* <virtuous wife and mother>. He asserts, definitively (p. 115): "[W]hat Catullus wrote was *Brixia, matronae mater amata meae* [<Brescia, beloved mother of my ma-tron>]."

At first blush, Giangrande's reasons for his emendation seem plausible (pp. 115-16):

> *Matrona* is used ironically by the poet, in tone with the whole of the poem: as a rule, the word implies the notion of virtuousness and marital fidelity, as but a glance at the lexica will show. *MAtronae MAter aMAta* is a type of alliteration much liked by Catullus [citing Schuster's *Index Verborum et Locutiorem,* but without providing examples] ..... [S]ince the poet has just mentioned a town-name, *Brixia*, the scribe automatically thought of another town-name, because his eye was misguided by the word that followed: the scribe, that is, thought of Catullus' own town .... Those who are conversant with textual criticism will immediately see that the "errore di pensiero" [<mental error>] – to use the Pasqualian term – on the part of the scribe was prompted by paleographical reasons: *atronae* and *ueronae* can in fact look practically the same.

> The *a* of the type "open above", used both in the half-uncial and in the early Carolingian...is often mistaken for a *u*;

in both the half uncial and the Carolingian minuscule ꞇ in which the horizontal stroke does not extend to the left looks very much like ꞓ in which the loop is filled by ink and has therefore the appearance of a horizontal stroke.

The beauty of this emendation resides in its school-book perfection, from the strictly *textkritisch* [<textual criticism>] point of view. The disappearing of the *m* can be explained precisely on the basis of the "lois psychologiques" [<psychological laws>] as expounded by Havet, Pasquali and Dain [with citation to Dain].

I am skeptical of "psychological laws" that state "precisely" that because the appearance of one town-name reminds a copyist of another town-name, an uncial *a* is mistaken for a *u*, a ꞇ is mistaken for an *e*, and the *m* that precedes an *a* is no longer visible to the copyist.

If 67:34 is viewed in isolation, Giangrande's case is stronger. But, neither textual criticism nor mental error explains why the Door would sing Brescia's praise in the *previous* two verses as well.

Giangrande continues (p. 117):

First of all, why the mention of Brixia at all? The answer is Lapalissian: so that the lady in question (and in consequence her cuckolded husband) could be identified by Catullus' readers.

Indeed. However, Giangrande *fails* to identify the lady and her cuckold as Clodia and Celer – or anyone else. Ironically, having just removed the song-poem's only reference to Verona, Giangrande almost immediately asserts (p. 118):

Poem 67 was relevant to Catullus and interesting for his readers in the sense that both Balbus and his family (including the unfortunate Caecilius) are likely to have been Veronese by birth, who had moved to Brixia.

He reaches this conclusion by drawing analogies to *Carmina* 17 and 59 xrl.us/bmfe9w. As indicated (p. 82 above), the latter (without ellipsis) begins: *bononiensis rufa rufulum fellat / uxor meneni* <Rufa of Bologna, Menenius's wife, fellates Little Rufie>. But here the name of the cuckoldress, her paramour, and their locale are the *first three words*. By contrast, in *Carmen* 67 the cuckoldress is unnamed in any of its 48 lines, the cuckold is ambiguously indicated to be the son of "Balbus" (a common nickname), and the locale is not mentioned until line 34. Even then, as Giangrande himself points out, the reference to the locale is "totally irrelevant to the context; indeed it is inopportune."

Carmen 17 is more on point: The location, *colonia*, is mentioned in lines 1 and 7, but since scholars have not been able to determine a location of such name, *colonia* may be a casual term, used by locals, for almost any recent or long-established colony of Rome.[121] And unlike 59, but like 67, in *Carmen* 17 Catullus's obloquy is focused mainly on the cuckold, in terms similar to those he employs in *Carmen* 83 xrl.us/bm ffdq, which are certainly directed at Clodia's husband, Celer:

> *insulsissimus est homo nec sapit pueri instar*
> *bimuli* .....   (17:12-13)

> The man is clueless, lacking the insight
> of a mere boy of two .....

> *lesbia mi praesente viro mala plurima dicit*
> *haec illi fatuo maxima laetitia est*
> *mule nihil sentis* .....   (83:1-3)

> Lesbia badmouths me in the worst way –
>   in front of her husband.
> (This is the greatest delight to that fat-head.)
> Impotent jackass, don't you *get it?!* .....

Hence, the song-poems analogous to 67, in terms of the object and tenor of their scorn, are 17 and 83 – not 59. To the extent that their respective locales are indicated in 17 and 59, it is in the first verse, and explicitly so, not three-quarters of the way into the song-poem – where it is, to repeat Giangrande's own terms, "totally irrelevant to the context; indeed, it is inopportune." Since *Lesbia* is named as such in 83, the cuckoldress and cuckold in 83 are clearly Clodia and Celer, and the locale, then, is implicitly Rome or Verona, because apparently the three of them are together when Clodia speaks insultingly of Catullus to her husband.

Echo Chamber

Thomson (2003, p. 470, n. 34) posits that the matter of *Veronae* versus *matronae* has been definitively resolved – in favor of *Veronae* – by an "echo" in a 9th century Latin squib by the Brescian theologian Ildemaro: "Billanovich 1988: 35-6 shows, from an echo in a much later text, that the true reading after all is *Veronae*."

With relevance to *Veronae* versus *matronae*, the gist of Billanovich's account is as follows:

The 20th century classicist/medievalist Bernhard Bischoff discovers in the Bavarian State Library a palimpsest on the surface of which is a 964 CE inventory of the possessions of a Brescian monastery (either San Faustino and Giovata, or San Faustino the Elder). Beneath this list can be discerned literary comments (only partially erased) that have been written, apparently in 845 CE, by the illustrious Brescian theologian Ildemaro. At that time, the Veronese monk Vitale is his guest, having been sent to Brescia by the Archdeacon of the Cathedral of Verona:

> ... *di ottenere il consulto del teologo insigne Ildemaro disputa che allora tormentava la diocesi di Verona, o piuttosto l'intera provincia ecclesiastica del patriarcato di Aquileia, se Adamo, padre dell'umanità, dopo la morte si salvò o fu dannato ...*

> ... to consult with the renowned theologian Ildemaro about the dispute that then raged in the Diocese of Verona, or rather the entire ecclesiastical province of the Patriarchate of Aquileia: whether Adam, the father of humanity, in death received salvation or damnation ...

During Vitale's visit, Billanovich continues, Ildemaro entertains his guest with readings from the 2nd century BCE Roman playwright of comedies Terence and with the wit of the late 1st century/early 2nd century CE satirist Juvenal. Ildemaro commemorates their recitals in a verse of his own.

Unfortunately, due to damage to the parchment, a number of words on the right side, as well as the ending, have been lost.

Billanovich's transcription of the Latin text, and my translation, follow:

Tempore iam brumae cum se sol vertit ad axe<<m>>,
alta petens celsi paulatim culmin<<a caeli>>,
verque sui primam captaret l . . . .
huc Verona suam matrem t. . . . .
mater quicquid abest gnatae ut mater. 5

Mox pariter primo Iuvenal . . . .
cuius nempe duos extremos carpere libros
egestas commentorum nos distulit egre.
Denique Terenti post dultia legimus acta,
sepe suis verbis iocundis atque facetis   10
nos quae fecerunt risum depromere magnum.

Et si mansisses, post hac studeremus in illis
quos adeo norunt perpauci tramite vero.
Quaeque tamen potui, tranquillo pectore, sodes,
exhibui, dum te libuit consistere mecum.   15
Abs me nunc abiens, recto nam calle Veron<<am>>
mentibus insertum. . . . .

Already in the season of the shortest day
    while the sun turns on its axis
gradually seeking the <<celestial>>
    summit high above,
and spring captures its first l ...
here, Verona her mother [accusative] ...
each mother [nominative] is away from a child
    as a mother [nominative] ...   5

Soon, side-by-side, first Juvenal ...
to choose two of whose last books
assuredly satisfied well our hunger for the ingenius.
Thereafter, we enjoyably recited acts from Terence –
whose funny and yet elegant writing   10
often caused us to laugh heartily.
And if you would have remained,
    after this we would have been studying
those who were very broadly acquainted with
    the very narrow path to truth.
Nevertheless, I furnished whatever I could,

with a contented heart,
while it was agreeable to you to stay with me.   15

From me now departing, straight forth
    by the stony road to Veron<<a>>
brought to mind ....

Billanovich then comments:

> *Ho già proposto che proprio Ildemaro abbia dettato ll car-*
> *me; immettendovi nel versi 4 e 5 un'eco sonora da Catullo,*
> *LXVII 31-34: perché nessun altro testo superstite della*
> *lettertura latina ci viene a dire che Brescia fu madre di*
> *Verona.*

> I have already suggested that Ildemaro has dictated his
> own poem; verses 4 and 5 merge into the sound of an
> echo from Catullus, 67:31-34: because **there is no other**
> **surviving text of Latin literature saying that Brescia**
> **was the mother of Verona.** [Emphasis added.]

Assuming that Billanovich is correct that Ildemaro entertain-
ing his Veronese guest, Vitale, is the context in which this
poem-fragment is written (Billanovich mentions that other
scholars view it as a teacher instructing a student), it seems
to this reader that perceiving a relationship between "Brescia,
beloved mother of *Verona mia*" and "here [*ie*, Brescia], Verona
her mother ... / each mother is away from a child as a mother ... " is more akin to free association than the sound of an
"echo". (Cp. Catullan echos in Shakespeare, Appendix A below.)

Whatever relevance this passage in a palimpsest may have to
Veronae vs *matronae* in 67:34, it is still unclear why the Door
of a house in Brescia (according to Giangrande's reading) or
in Verona (in most other readings) would sing Brescia's prai-
ses for three verses to an audience more likely to be Roman or
Veronese than Brescian (though the last is not inconceivable).

Further, why would Catullus wait until line 34 to have the Door
indicate its location, in light of the fact that the respective
locales in the three other song-poems of Catullus's *Cuckold*
Quartet (17, 59, 67, and 83) are all immediately identified?

Examining 67:34, not in isolation but in the context of the two preceding verses, we read:

> *brixia chinea suppositum specula*
> *flavus quam molli praecurrit flumine mella*
> *brixia veronae mater amata meae*   (32-34)

> *Brescia*, set 'neath China Hill look-out,
> where the yellow Mello river gently flows;
> *Brescia*, beloved mother of *Verona mia*

To this reader, these verses are not only "totally irrelevant" and "inopportune" – they border on the absurd. As already noted, Giangrande (p. 113) asks (in support of eliminating Verona from the reading): How would the Door know "local antiquarian lore" about Verona's Brescian origins? And, as Skinner (2003, p.49) observes, there is no reason to believe the Door has "organs of vision" – yet here the Door (*incorrectly*, apparently) describes the topography of a city several days' journey away.

Perhaps evidence cannot be found of a Chinea Hill, or a look-out built atop it, because neither ever existed. The river Mello does not run *through* Brescia, and to call river water *flavus* <flaxen, thus yellow or golden> may not *necessarily* be a compliment.

Mock Poet

Catullus has no motive to mock poetic pretensions on the part of the Door, but he does have such motive with respect to the new man in Clodia's life, the Caecilius II to whom readers /listeners were introduced in *Carmen* 35:1 as *tenero meo sodali* <touching poet, my comrade [*ie*, in ClubClodia]>.

Giangrande (p. 125, n. 144) discusses his and other scholars' puzzlement over the purpose of this poem-within-a-poem, including Baehrens's characterization of it as *inrisio lepidissima* <risibly 'ultra-sophisticated'>. To my eyes, Catullus's 'invitation' to Caecilius II, *Carmen* 35, drips with sarcasm, and 67:32-34 follows-up with *a lampoon of Caecilius II's efforts as a poet*.

Now that *Carmen* 67 is teetering on the ludicrous, the Interlocutor attempts to restore a semblance of plausibility by feigning skepticism – not at the absurdity of a slave-girl Door knowing another city's history and topography, or her having the ability to extemporaneously recite risible verse about same, but rather how she would know about the one subject *any* slave-girl could be expected to know well: *the gossip circulating about her Mistress.*

> *dixerit hic aliquis quid tu istaec ianua nosti*
> *cui nunquam domini limine abesse licet*
> *nec populum auscultare sed hic suffixa tigillo*
> *tantum operire soles aut aperire domum*   (37-40)

At *this*, someone might say, "How did *you* learn these
    things, Miss Door,
who never has license to absent the Master's threshold,
nor hear *townspeople?* Instead, you've been affixed to the
    lintel *here*,
so your function is to admit (or to *not admit!*) to the home.

Green comments (2005, p. 250):

> The objection severely strains our suspension of disbelief,
> even though chiefly directed at the door's immobility (which
> was never in doubt). But the objector is also represented
> as addressing a door that, he supposes, can't hear gossip
> (39).

Bragging Rights

Catullus's real purpose here is not to make it seem credible that a talkative slave-girl Door, though immobile in Verona, is nonetheless all but omniscient about Brescia, but rather to reveal the ultimate source of the juicy dish about Clodia: Clodia *herself:*

> *saepe illam audivi furtiva voce loquentem*
> *solam cum ancillis haec sua flagitia*
> *nomine dicentem quos diximus ut pote quae mi*
> *speraret nec linguam esse nec auriculam*   (41-44)

I often heard *her* talking – in a *furtive* voice
with only slave-girls present – about her *outrageousness*,
naming the names we spoke about.
(She naturally would have been hoping me to be with
    neither tongue nor ear).

Giangrande here comments (p. 121):

> [W]hereas it would be natural for the lady to talk with her *ancillae* [<slave-girls>] about her present *flagitia* [<outrageousness>], i.e. the *adulteria* which she is committing after her marriage, why should she mention her *past flagitia*, i.e. her incest, to them?

Giangrande's solution (pp. 127-28) is to collapse the narrative to a single locale, Brescia, where "the door has heard the *ancillae* report to their *matrona* rumours which they had collected in town, rumours about her incest and about her *adulteria*."

Here, again, the necessity of identifying the woman is exemplified: If she is Clodia, Catullus may well have heard about her past affairs in Brescia from Clodia's own lips (or those of Cornelius Nepos; *see* Appendix E). She may have told these tales to taunt him, arouse him, or both. Or, he may have heard the stories from her slave-girls. (About whom, other than Clodia, would Catullus know so much detailed gossip that is being spread by slave-girls about their Mistress?)

Moreover, if the woman is Clodia, Giangrande's question is answered: For what reason would Clodia *not* brag to her slave-girls about past frolics? Whether Clodia is viewed in the traditionalist manner as a wealthy widow-run-wild, or in the postmodern manner of Clodia/Lesbia as figment of the forensic imagination of Cicero and the poetic imagination of Catullus, this reader finds no reason to believe that Clodia, real or fictive, is at all reticent about being *Clodia!* On the contrary, Cicero, who as an upper-middle-class striver is obsessed with maintaining appearances for appearances' sake, seems on the verge of apoplexy as he thunders loud enough to be heard by the outer *corona* <ring> of spectators in the Roman Forum:

> *nihilne igitur illa vicinitas redolet nihilne hominum fama nihil baiae denique ipsae loquuntur illae vero non loquuntur solum verum etiam personant huc unius mulieris libidinem esse prolapsam ut ea non modo solitudinem ac tenebras atque haec flagitiorum integumenta non quaerat sed in turpissimis rebus frequentissima celebritate et clarissima luce laetetur* (*Pro Caelio* 20 xrl.us/bmh9hg)

Accordingly, doesn't her noisome neighborhood, doesn't all the talk, and lastly *Palm Beach*[122] – don't they speak for *themselves?* In truth, they not only *say* it, they veritably *shout* that the libido of one fallen woman to be such that, not in a *private* manner in the *shadows* and not even seeking *concealment* of her outrageous acts, but with the utmost frequency she *delights* in acts of the greatest turpitude in *broad daylight!*

Further still, if Clodia is the mystery woman of *Carmen* 67, then the *magnas ... lites* is surely the trial of Caelius. Hence her husband, Celer, has been dead for three years – leaving Catullus without reason to fear the disclosures of 67 would subject Clodia (or himself) to retribution from Celer.

A Belly of Lies

The tall, temperamental, russet-browed litigant of lines 45-47 has already been discussed (pp. 44-45 above). What remains is the final line, the juiciest dish of all:

falsum mendaci ventre puerperium (48)

against a *belly of lies* over a *miscarried* boy-birth!

Since no one, not even slave-girls, can know with certainty all that has actually occurred between Clodia and Caelius, the slave-girls have likely disseminated multiple versions of the precise details. Thus, in this last line Catullus uses language appropriately ambiguous: *mendaci* <lies> is clear enough, but it is paired with *ventre* <belly, stomach, womb>.

Neither a belly nor a womb can literally lie. Is Catullus referring here to an (unintentionally) 'false pregnancy', or to a (dishonestly) 'simulated pregnancy' xrl.us/bm4xyx? A false (or less than certain) attribution of paternity to Caelius?

Falsum <false>, as in English, may mean innocently mistaken, or intentionally untrue. Etymologically, *puerperium* combines *puer* <boy> and *pariere* <give birth to>, but generally applies to any birth. Here, however, Clodia's hopes for a male heir are the crux of the matter.

And yet, whether from innocent error, intent to deceive, or a misleading medical condition, what is a *false* boy-birth? The conclusion of a false pregnancy? The unmasking of a dishonest attribution of paternity?

Or, is it a *miscarriage* induced by an abortifacient, perhaps administered via lubrication of an artificial substitute for the male sex organ, presented in the type of characteristically-shaped *pyxis* <box> immediately recognizable as such to a holiday crowd in the Roman Forum? (Cp. *Pro Caelio* 61, 63-5, 69; Quintilian, *Institutio Oratoria* 6.3.25 xrl.us/bm4yoq; Wiseman 1974, pp. 170-75.)

The Razor's Edge

To repeat a quote by Russell (1924, p. 160): "Whenever possible, substitute constructions out of known entities for inferences to unknown entities."

If Ockham's Razor, as formulated by Russell, is applied, there remains only one "face" of Sappho, who is *both* the erotic and poetic Muse of Catullus. He thus names as *Lesbia* the Sappho incarnate of his poetry, because Clodia plays *both* roles in his corporeal existence.

In accord, there is only one *Lesbius* who is *pulcher* (79:1): P Clodius Pulcher; and only one *P Clodius* in Cicero's lexicon: Clodia's brother Clodius. Clodius has only one sister named *Clodia:* Clodia Metelli (*see* Appendix D). Hence, when Apuleius writes (*Apol* 10), in his own defense, that Catullus called Clodia *Lesbia,* there can be only one referent: Clodia Metelli.

By *any* reading (so far), there is only one *Marcus Tullius* (49:2) to whom Catullus would address song-poem 49: Marcus Tullius Cicero – from whose private correspondence and trial transcript, *Pro Caelio,* both Clodia Metelli and Marcus Caelius Rufus are forever inseparable. Hence, Catullus's *Caelius* (58:1; 100:1,5,7) and *Rufus* (69:2; 77:1) are referents to only one person: Marcus Caelius Rufus.

To further avoid the unnecessary creation of otherwise unattested entities: The *Cornelius* to whom Catullus dedicates the *Passer* (1:3), the one whose secret Catullus promises to keep (102:4), and the one he reveals (67:35) as an early lover of the eventual wife of the son of *Balbus* is only one person: Cornelius Nepos.

There likewise is only one *puella* in 35:8 and 35:16, and since she is *Sapphica* (35:16), and since Sappho is born on the Isle of Lesbos, this *puella* is Lesbia, and thus her *Caecilius*, at least in part, alludes to Celer, the one and only husband of Clodia/Lesbia.

There are, though, *two* people named *Caecilius* in the *Liber Catulli* (both of whom are intimates of Clodia Metelli). However, it is not the case that but one of them is referred to in 35, while only the other is referred to in 67. As Thomson observes (n. 110 below), Catullus's allusion to *Caecilius* in 35:2,18 is the same allusion as appears in 67:9. Since, *Caecilius* is part of Celer's full name, the association with *him* is unavoidable.

Catullus's reference to *Novi ... / Comi moenia* <the walls of New Como> (35:3-4) is superfluous as an indication of Caecilius's location, because the words that follow immediately *Lariumque litus* <loosely: the beach at Lake Como> describe virtually the same locale. The double-reference to Caecilius's location instead is made to specify the song-poem's *time-frame:* Caesar establishes New Como in the spring of 59 BCE bit.ly/PwYUqo – *after* Celer's untimely death.

Hence, *Caecilius* is a double-*entendre* to both Celer and the *newest* 'New Poet' in Clodia Metelli's life. This Caecilian clansman of Celer has inherited the house of Celer's father in Verona, because Clodia has not produced a male heir. But note: Catullus is *not* here using the *same* name in *different* senses from one song-poem to another.

As already indicated (p. 48 above), in the last two lines of the first song-poem of the *Passer* (1:9-10), Catullus prays that his little book of 'trifles' will be read by future generations. He surely knows which people will come to mind for future readers when they read names such as *Caelius*, *Rufus*, *Caecilius*, and *Marcus Tullius* – particularly in the context of his work as a whole. Conversely, Catullus would just as surely realize that to use the *same* name to identify *different* people would significantly undermine his goal of communicating his meaning to future readers (ditto Cicero, re: *P Clodius*).

Further, a reading that accepts *Caelius, Caecilius, P Clodius, et al*, as the same persons, respectively, everywhere these names appear engenders far fewer maddeningly confusing details, riddles, and enigmas than alternative readings.

Separating Fact From Faction

There is the irreducible fact that Clodia Metelli, notwithstanding undoubted foreknowledge of the nature of the attacks Cicero would make on her character, nonetheless testifies in open court that Marcus Caelius Rufus has attempted to poison her. This must be due to more than "a few little words". And, all evidence suggests that Clodia's (and Clodius's) politics are in radical opposition to those of their brothers; hence, there is no indication that the prosecution of Caelius was brought at the behest of Clodia's other brothers.

There is an absence of surviving testimonia linking Pompey to violence against the Alexandrian emissaries, and none that links Caelius to Pompey *or* the violence.

There are two *carmina*, 69 and 77, that appear to allude to Caelius's reputation as a poisoner of women (*see* p. 38 above).

Finally, there is *Carmen* 67, which 1) explicitly employs *Caecilius* (67:9), a clan name of Clodia Metelli's husband; 2) implicitly embeds her husband's nickname, *Celer* (67:24); 3) uses the nickname of an ancestor of Clodia, *Caecus* (67:25); 4) uses the nickname of one of the prosecutors of Caelius in *Pro Caelio, Balbus* (67:3); 5) provides a verbal description that matches Caelius's appearance and temperament (67:46-7); and 6) has as its subtext a woman's failed attempt to bear a male heir, resulting in a great trial involving this philanderer who looks like Caelius.

Concluding Remarks

In addition to what I feel is the greatly increased clarity afforded by the application of Ockham's Razor in readings of both Catullus and Cicero, a few more observations are offered:

Foremost among them, as what might be called a meta-concern: Any reading that implies, however obliquely, that Catullus has failed to achieve one of his major artistic goals (or, for that matter, that Cicero does not know how to properly present a criminal defense) ought be entertained only with extreme caution.

Second, literary theory is best employed in order to illuminate literature, rather than *vice versa.*

Third, the 'low hanging fruit' of textual emendation has already been picked. Further emendation, in most instances, is likely to produce more questions than answers. (Nonetheless, I have proposed an emendation of my own. *See* n. 89 below.)

Fourth, the more a translation varies from a literal rendering, the more opportunities arise for misreading the author's intent.

The present volume begins, in part (*see* p. 1 above):

> This monograph presents a reading of *Carmen* 67 that is unique in several respects: 1) the major characters are all identified (as personages well-known to Catullus's circle); 2) song-poem 67 is integrated into the other 'Lesbia poems'; 3) 67's allusions to both *Carmen* 35 ("Summon Caecilius") and Cicero's *Pro Caelio* are demonstrated (thereby making the identification of the pseudonymous *Lesbia* as Clodia Metelli more apparent yet); 4) TW Hillard's hypothesis regarding Celer's paternity is confirmed; 5) 67's 'Cornelius connection' to song-poems 1 and 102 is drawn; 6) the several peculiarities of the poem-within-a-poem (lines 32-34) are explained; and 7) with as much clarity as 67's inherent allusiveness will allow, the *real* reason Clodia brings a prosecution against her ex-lover, Marcus Caelius Rufus, is revealed.

Still unresolved is the identity of one of Clodia's Brescian lovers, *Postumius* (67:35). Regarding a *Postumia* who is in attendance at what is likely a literary stag-party, and who commands the pouring of cups of *undiluted* wine though she is already *ebriosa acina ebriosiori* <more inebriated than a drunken grape> (27:4), Green observes (2005, p. 305):

> As often with Catullus ... it looks as though we have to do here with a brother and sister, probably from Brescia, where the name is common, and thus part of Catullus's Cisalpine circle of friends.

(Yet perhaps there is again but *one* individual, Postumius/a, who happens to be playing the 'party-girl' at the all-male gathering.)

In closing, I thank all of the readers who have had the patience to journey thus far into my little book, and I hope that at least a few will find that it has contributed 'some-things' to the ongoing conversation about *Carmen* 67.

Appendix A: *Echos Upon the Avon*

Jacob Blevins (p. 39 ff. xrl.us/bmeo5w) notes:

> Two of Shakespeare's contemporaries link him to Catullus .... [Francis] Meres writes: "As ... Horace and Catullus among the Latines are the best Lyrick poets: so in this faculty the best among our poets are Spencer (who excelleth in all kinds), Daniel, Drayton, Shakespeare, Bretton." Also, Richard Carew ... attempts to glorify English writers by comparing the great English ones to corresponding classical writers .... [Carew] writes: "Will you read Virgill? take the Earl of Surrey: Catullus? Shakespeare and Marlowes fragment."

Cp. In fair Verona, where we lay our scene,
From ancient grudge break to new mutiny (*Romeo and Juliet*, Prologue, 2-3 xrl.us/bmrrwu)

Born in Verona .. (*The Taming of the Shrew*, I, ii, 190 xrl.us/bmrvrn)

The ship is here put in,
A Veronesa ... (*Othello*, II, i, 25-6 xrl.us/bmrxbj)

Myself was from Verona banished
For practising to steal away a lady (*Two Gentlemen of Verona*, IV, i, 1599-1600 xrl.us/bmrrxv)

Edwin Reed (pp. 179-80) draws the following parallels (translations Reed's):

Catullus:

> *qui nunc it per iter tenebricosum*
> *illuc unde negant redire quemquam*

The dark journey whence they say no one returns.
(*Carmen* 3:11-2 xrl.us/bmfnm3)

Shakespeare:

> The undiscover'd country from whose bourn
> No traveller returns... (*Hamlet*, III, i, 79-80 xrl.us/bmrvss)

Catullus:

si sapiet viam vorabit

If he be wise, he will devour the way ... (*Carmen* 35:7 xrl.us/bmfb35)

Shakespeare:

He seemed in running to devour the way. (*2 Henry IV*, I, i, 99 xrl.us/bmrt8d)

Catullus:

si tibi non cordi fuerant conubia nostra
[saeva quod horrebas prisci praecepta parentis]
attamen in vestras potuisti ducere sedes
quae tibi iucundo famularer serva labore ...

If our marriage had not been agreeable to you [...]
you could have taken me to your home, where, as your maid, I would cheerfully have served you. (*Carmen* 64: 158, 160-61 xrl.us/bmfcdp)

Shakespeare:

I am your wife, if you will marry me;
If not, I'll die your maid: to be your fellow
You may deny me; but I'll be your servant ... (*The Tempest*, III, i, 83-5 xrl.us/bmrufp)

Catullus:

... quae cum pulcherrima tota est
tum omnibus una omnis surripuit veneres

[Lesbia] is most beautiful of all, having stolen all graces from all others. (*Carmen* 86:5-6 xrl.us/bmfcgd)

Shakespeare:

Nature made all graces dear,
When she did starve the general world beside
And prodigally gave them all to you. (*Love's Labor Lost*, II, i, 493-5 xrl.us/bmrugj)

Appendix B: *The Sound and the Fury of Brotherly Love*

The scholarly consensus is that the second prosecutor, P Clodius, is not Clodia's brother. Thus, Austin (p. 83, n. 3; also p. 155): "Atratinus' *subscriptores* [<co-counsel>] were P. Clodius and L. Herennius Balbus. It is unlikely that the former is Clodia's notorious brother"; Wiseman (1987, p. 72): "If we are right to infer that [P. Clodius] was a client of the patrician Claudii ..."; Gruen (p. 307): "[A] certain P. Clodius inveighed solidly against Caelius' moral shortcomings. That will not have been the tribune of 58 ... it was more likely a lesser member of the *gens* or a client"; Tatum (p. 209): "Atratinus was assisted by a certain P. Clodius – not the aedile of 56 of course but rather his client ... "; Hejduk (p. 80, n. 36): "This is almost certainly not Publius Clodius Pulcher, but some more obscure member of the family"; Elizabeth Keitel and Jane W Crawford (p. 12): "P. Clodius: probably a freedman of Clodius Pulcher ... "

The arguments of Austin and subsequent commentators, and my counter-arguments, are too lengthy to set forth here in their entirety, but they will be detailed in my forthcoming biography of Clodia. Suffice it, for now, to point out that Clodius has an important choice on April 4, 56 BCE: *either* 1) find a stand-in for his role as Aedile in presiding over the Megalenses Games, *or* 2) leave his most beloved sister to the tender mercies of Cicero, to be defended against Cicero's attacks on her character by a mere family retainer – who is to use Clodius's own name.

As noted, the second choice has been the one adopted by many scholars (but *see* p. 121 below), notwithstanding that *p clodius* is exactly as Clodia's brother's name, and his alone, is styled in many of Cicero's other surviving works (including his private correspondence). Moreover, no other attestation exists for this supposed stand-in's existence (ditto, the "touching poet" of *Carmen* 35), even though Cicero acerbically mentions, mid-trial, that he and *this* particular *p clodius* have a 'past':

nam p clodius amicus meus cum se gravissime vehemen-
tissimeque iactaret et omnia inflammatus ageret tristissi-
mis verbis voce maxima tametsi probabam eius eloquen-
tiam tamen non pertimescebam aliquot enim in causis eum
videram frustra litigantem (*Pro Caelio* 27 xrl.us/bif6sk)

As for Publius Clodius, my 'pal', he has been hurling himself about, gesticulating with the utmost gravity and vehe-
mence, totally inflamed, shouting the angriest words, in
the loudest voice. Although I do commend his eloquence,
nevertheless I'm not worrying; in fact, I have seen him liti-
gating deceptively *several* cases.

Cp. Cicero, *Atticus* 2.22.1 xrl.us/bmioid: *volitat furit nihil ha-*
bet certi multis denuntiat <[Clodius] flies about, he rages, he
can't make up his mind, he makes many threats>. *See* also
"sound and fury" reference to Clodius in n. 38 below.

In addition, the identification of the second prosecution speaker as our Clodius makes sense of this otherwise superfluous
passage:

quam quidem partem accusationis admiratus sum et mo-
leste tuli potissimum esse atratino datam neque enim de-
cebat neque aetas illa postulabat neque id quod animum
advertere poteratis pudor patiebatur optimi adulescentis
in tali illum oratione versari vellem aliquis ex vobis robus-
tioribus hunc male dicendi locum suscepisset aliquanto
liberius et fortius et magis more nostro refutaremus istam
male dicendi licentiam (*Pro Caelio* 7 xrl.us/bikuki)

In fact, how surprised I have been at the greatest portion
of the slander having been given to (and having been un-
comfortably conveyed by) *Atratinus*.

Indeed, neither is it befitting, nor to be expected at his
age, that you [*ie*, Clodia and Clodius] have had the power
to twist his mind. The embarrassment endured by this
most upstanding young man – to have involved *him* in that
speech!

I would have wished one of the more *seasoned* among
you here [*ie*, Clodius] had undertaken the slanderous
utterances instead.

In other words, Cicero here relishes aloud the thought of replying in kind to an attack by *Clodius* regarding Caelius's moral lapses – particularly those in relation to *Clodia*.

Of special note, Skinner (2010, p. 165, n. 30) writes:

> Previously I suggested that Caelius's landlord was the secondary accuser in the trial rather than the tribune of 58 [Clodia's brother Clodius] (Skinner 1983: 282 n. 23). However, valuable income would more likely be in the hands of the nobility themselves, not their clients.

Since *p clodius* is Cicero's styling of the name of Clodia's brother in his capacity as the owner of Caelius's apartment, the second prosecutor (whose name is styled identically) must likewise be Clodia's brother Publius Clodius.

Appendix C: *Animation Pre-Pixar*

Wikipedia defines *paraclausithyron* thus <u>xrl.us/bk3jtx</u>:

> A para[c]lausithyron typically places a lover outside his mistress's door, desiring entry. In Greek poetry, the situation is connected to the *komos*, the revels of young people outdoors following intoxication at a symposium. Callimachus uses the situation to reflect on self-control, passion, and free will when the obstacle of the door is removed.

Paul Murgatroyd (p. 472), regarding the applicability of the *paraclausithyron* motif to *Carmen* 67:

> Surely it is at least equally possible [*contra* Copley 1956, pp. 47-51] that the employment of the locked-out lover's serenade for extensive *diffamatio* [<defamation>] concerning adulterous and explicitly sexual misdemeanours was an innovation by the New Poet himself. In either case, however derivative or original 67 is in this respect, the learned Catullus would of course have been familiar with the literary παραχλαυσίτυρου [<*paraclausithyron*>], his (literary) piece naturally invites comparison with that form, and when one does compare them one finds that the twists to and variations on the stock locked-out lover's serenade are too obvious and extensive to be accidental and that Catullus' piece virtually amounts to an inversion of the standard form (and I might add that all of this shows a cleverness and complexity that one would hardly expect in a non-literary context).

Thus, consistent with his overall program, Catullus here melds the baser metals of Roman lust and greed into high literary form, Greek in origin.

Catullus's animation of the otherwise inanimate is not found solely in 67. In song-poem 4 <u>xrl.us/bmx5u2</u>, his sailing ship brags of being the fleetest. Catullus orders the papyrus upon which he writes 35 to summon Caecilius (II) to Verona (*see* pp. 71-75 above). In *Carmen* 36 <u>xrl.us/bmfhyh</u>, Catullus commands a work by Volusius, which he (twice) describes as *cacata* <'cah-cah'> (36:1,20), to self-immolate. He marshals hendecasyllables xrl.us/bmxwsx in song-poem 42 xrl.us/bm xwtq to conduct noisy street demonstrations demanding that an unnamed 'brazen hussy' (who else but Clodia?) return his *codicilli* <wax tablets> – upon which he presumably has written (what else?) 'Lesbia poems'. In 66 xrl.us/bmfcij, a lamenting lock of Queen Berenice's hair ascends into the heavens to become the constellation Coma Berenices xrl.us/bmxump.

In 55:7 xrl.us/bmxwvd, Catullus engages in saucy banter with the *femellas* <'girlies'> (a word unique, in surviving literary usage, to Song-poem 55) assembled at Pompey's Portico xrl.us/bmxwwr.

It has long been assumed that these *femellae* congregate there to offer their time and companionship to generous gentlemen callers. However, Molly Pasco-Pranger's insightful reading proposes that the *femellae* in question are *statues* of *Muses*. (Some of the portico's statuary, unlike the purported *femellae* of that time, still exist.)

In combination with the five foregoing song-poems, and in light of Callimachus (and other Greeks) having written verses about talking statues of Muses, along with 67 as caricature of a Callimachean *paraclausithyron*, Pasco-Pranger's reading of 55 as a caricature of the Muse's-statue-talks-to-Poet motif is irresistible. My own inclination, and I think Pasco-Pranger's, is to view her reading as inclusive of the traditional reading.

Appendix D: *"Clodia" – The One and* Only

Regarding the correct names of our Clodia and Clodius (and their near relatives), the profusion of variant spellings among surviving manuscripts of ancient sources is well presented by Walter Allen, Jr in "Claudius or Clodius?", and by Andrew M Riggsby's subsequent "Clodius/Claudius".

Before reaching a conclusion about a revisionist identification of an ancient personage, readers might enjoy playwright Tom Stoppard's mordant musings on the uncertainty of the Catullan text, which of course apply equally to the existing manuscripts of other ancient authors: xrl.us/bibt88. To Stoppard's account, James L Butrica adds (Skinner, ed., 2007, p. 14):

> "Jowett" can be criticized on some minor points: he neglects causes of corruption other than scribal error, ignores the 'secondary' tradition [*ie,* quotations of Catullus provided by ancient and medieval scholars], elides the considerable scholarly activity that intervened between the rediscovery and first publication, and in general downplays *the element of sheer uncertainty that surrounds the whole enterprise of recovering an ancient text...* [Emphasis added.]

Though modern scholars refer to *each* of the three sisters of P Clodius as "Clodia" (Riggsby p. 118, n. 6), nonetheless there is only the sketchiest of evidence that *one* of Clodia Metelli's sisters is also called "Clodia", and *none* with respect to her other sister.

Plutarch, in a single passage (*Lucullus* 38.1 xrl.us/bmr5e5), does name as "Clodia" (perhaps because he was an 'early modern' scholar?) one of Clodia Metelli's two sisters: the unfaithful wife of Lucullus until their 66 BCE divorce (when Catullus is barely old enough to wear a *toga virilis* <roughly: a man's business suit>). Lucullus is the military commander against whom Clodius mutinies in 67 BCE. During his trial for *Incestus* in 61 BCE, Clodius is accused of committing incest with *this* sister, while she is still married to Lucullus (cf. pp. 12, 17 above).

However, Plutarch writes in Greek, and Allen (p. 107) observes regarding a reference in Greek to P Clodius's (adamantly
anti-populist) brother Appius as "Clodius": "Sturtevant's list
of transliterations shows that in this matter the Greeks were
so inconsistent that their evidence has no value." Further, in
his only passage that references *all three* of P Clodius's
sisters, Plutarch refers *solely* to Metellus Celer's wife as "Clodia" (*Cicero* 29.3-4 xrl.us/bmr9cg).

Thus, though scholars continue to refer to her as "Clodia Luculli", a likely more accurate appellation is "Claudia Luculli".

Cicero's references to P Clodius's inept brother Gaius, also, as
"Clodius" (*Atticus* 3.17.1 xrl.us/bmsgvs and 4.15.2 xrl.us/bms
gv2) ought be viewed in the light of Cicero's irrepressible sarcasm.

In a letter to Metellus Celer (*Familiares* 5.2.6 xrl.us/bifmmi),
Cicero refers to Celer's wife as "Claudia". But note Cicero's
qualification, *uxore tua* <your wife>, implying that her sisters,
too, are named "Claudia".

In an exchange of letters with Mark Antony (*Atticus* 14.13A.2
xrl.us/bmwknw and 14.13B.4 xrl.us/bmwkn4), both men refer
to P Clodius's son as "Clodius". But, other ancient sources
(*see* Riggsby p. 117, n. 1) indicate that P Clodius's son pre-
fers his ancestors' name, "Claudius", and that similarly P
Clodius's daughter is known as "Claudia".

There is even a source stating that some call *P Clodius* "Claudius" (Cassius Dio, *Historiae Romanae* 36.14.4 xrl.us/bmsgm
z). In this regard, readers might note that Copley (1949 p.
245, n. 1-2) twice misspells the name of a classicist of his own
generation, Gennaro Perrotta (*see* p. 80 above) – and does so
twice again in n. 3-4 of his p. 247. Conceivably the root of
this misspelling is the source document Copley is working
from. However it has been introduced, the misspelling has
survived the prepublication vetting process of The American
Philological Association, which surely is more rigorous than
that imposed upon ancient and medieval copyists over the
centuries. (Notwithstanding the many hours I have expended
in checking and rechecking the present work, I would be very

surprised if there were not outright errors, including mis-spellings, still lurking hither and thither herein.)

In spite of the misspellings in Copley's article (or mine), it is to be hoped that 2,000 years hence, it will not be inferred that there are two distinct 20th century classicists, one nam-ed Gennaro Perrotta; the other, G Perotta.

Suetonius (*Tiberius* 2.2 xrl.us/bmsaxu) informs us that the single member of the proud and haughty Claudian dynasty to enter into *populist* politics is P Clodius – in order to attack Cicero via election to the office of Tribune (*see* pp. 18, 20-1 above). Cicero unambiguously attaches Clodia Metelli to Clo-dius's political aims (*eg, Quintus Frater* 2.3.2 xrl.us/biiveq); none of the ancient authorities do so with respect to either of her sisters.

Wiseman's fascinating speculation (1974, p. 104) that poly-math C Julius Hyginus is Apuleius's *source* for identifying Catullus's Lesbia as "Clodia" begs the fact that Apuleius uses her *first* name only (and those of the real-life lovers of three of Catullus's imitators in the generation that follows; *see* p. 50 above). Since Apuleius is trying to convince his readers, by reference to these four prior examples, that his own use of pseudonyms is blameless, he obviously has chosen names with which his contemporary readers are already familiar. Thus, Apuleius identifies Lesbia only as "Clodia" in all likeli-hood because, even two centuries afterward, no one *other* than Clodia Metelli would have been thought by his generation to be Catullus's Lesbia.

Yet, Wiseman (1969, p. 56; similarly, 1987, p. 2, quoted on p. 86 above) hypothesizes:

> If we had a speech against Clodius from 61 B.C. instead of one in defence of Caelius from 56, the identification of Clodia [*sic*] Luculli as Lesbia would seem as self-evident as that of Clodia Metelli has appeared to many modern scholars.

Even if Lucullus's ex-wife, too, were known as "Clodia", and even if a transcript of Clodius's trial for *Incestus* were to have survived to the present day, Wiseman's hypothetical "instead of one in defence of Caelius" is unarguably counterfactual:

We do have Cicero's *Pro Caelio*, and since we have it, Apuleius and his contemporaries undoubtedly have it. Therefore, were the wives of Metellus and Lucullus *both* named "Clodia" (all the more so if *all three* sisters were), Apuleius would need to have specified which sister he is identifying as Lesbia (cp. Cicero's letter to Celer, p. 125 above), or assume his readers would know she is the *most* (in)famous of the three sisters.

Lucullus's ex-wife is barely more than a footnote to the trial of her brother Clodius. Whereas, Cicero insures that Clodia Metelli is the 'main event' in what is one of the most sensational trials of the ancient world (*see* p. 45 above and n. 55 below), including his implying that, unlike either of her sisters, Clodia poisoned to death her husband – a man of Consular rank. Cicero, with a subsequent assist from Plutarch, fairly or unfairly makes certain that the most notorious of the three sisters, for all time to come, is Clodia Metelli.

Evidence associating the name "Clodia" with Clodia Metelli includes Cicero's *Pro Caelio* and a number of his private letters spanning sixteen years. The latter include, in my reading, the two letters of 49 BCE (*Atticus* 9.6.3 xrl.us/bmsk5b and 9.9.2 xrl.us/bmsk6k) identifying "Clodia" as Cicero's conduit for information (a role Clodia Metelli has been playing all along) about the mass exodus of aristocrats from Rome to Greece in the wake of Pompey's fleeing there from Caesar.

Lucullus's former wife may have accompanied her, as do a number of Clodia Metelli's other relatives (Wiseman 1974, pp. 113-4). But, there is no reason to suppose that Cicero would use the same name, "Clodia", to indicate a *different* source of political intelligence than she who has been such all along.

As already discussed (p. 78 above), allusions to Clodia Metelli as Catullus's "Lesbia" include (when read in conjunction with *Pro Caelio*) the two song-poems associating her with a "Caelius", another two linking her to a "Rufus", and two that connect her to a "Caecilius", as well as Catullus's 'thank-you' note to Cicero. There is evidence of no such allusions in Catullus's work to either of her sisters.

By contrast, the sole evidence (if it be even that) attaching the name "Clodia" to either of the other sisters is the above-cited reference by Plutarch, of questionable transliteration, to the wife of Lucullus, and *marginalia* to Cicero's two letters of 49 BCE written some seven centuries later by the unnamed Bobbio scholiast, which even Wiseman (1974, p. 114, n. 54) impliedly discounts. Wiseman himself (1974, pp. 141-43) observes that the manuscript of Plutarch known as *N* disagrees with other manuscripts with reference to some *twenty* names: "Some of them are demonstrably wrong .... some of them correct [*eg*, 'Atticus' instead of 'Attius']" and some "we do not know".

The evidence, taken as whole, that Apuleius identifies Lesbia as Clodia *Metelli* is overwhelming; contrary 'evidence' borders on the fanciful.

But then, Albert Einstein reputedly remarked that in science there is no such thing as *too much* skepticism. Perhaps that is likewise true of classical philology.

Appendix E: *Cornelius Nepos –*
The Godfather?

Copley (1957, p. xiii) writes of the New Poets:

> Their leader was [Publius] Valerius Cato, teacher, scho-
> lar, and critic, whose critical judgment – at least so one
> of them says – was enough to make or break a poet.

Whigham (p. 232) speculates: "[Valerius Cato] may well have
been the original source of the new movement in poetry."

Yet, in his more-bawdy-than-usual *Carmen* 56 xrl.us/bm56zm,
Catullus addresses Valerius Cato as a *chum* (56:1,3), perhaps
using him as a stand-in for a bigger target: the sternly pru-
dish Cato the Younger (*see* Green, p. 313). Whereas, the tone
of the dedicatory *Carmen* 1, while merry, is nonetheless clearly an act of *gratitude* to Cornelius Nepos.

I think it very likely that Clodia is 'Great Mother' to the New
Poets, from Catullus's perspective at the least. *See,* for exam-
ple, 68B:135 xrl.us/bmhhd2 *tamen etsi uno non est contenta
Catullo* <And, though [Lesbia] is not content with *just one*
'Catullus'...>, implying *other* New Poets caught her fancy.

Similarly, it would be unsurprising if biographer/historian
Cornelius Nepos, again from Catullus's perspective, were the
'Godfather' of the New Poets.

In parallel with Thomson's observation that the *Caecilius* who
is the 'sensitive poet' of song-poem 35 is not improbably also
the contemporaneous occupant of the House of Balbus in 67
(*see* n. 110 below), and with the majority view that the *Rufus*
of 69 and 77, and the *Caelius* of 58 and 100, are the Marcus
Caelius Rufus of *Pro Caelio*, and also with Skinner's (and my
own) reading of *P Clodius* in *Pro Caelio* as the *P Clodius* of
Cicero's other public speeches and his private correspondence: The *Cornelius Nepos* who is the dedicatee of song-
poem 1:3 xrl.us/bmw2e5 is not unlikely the *Cornelius* who is
one of Clodia's premarital lovers in 67:35, as well as the *Cornelius* whose 'secret' Catullus swears 'by Harpocrates' he will
keep (102:4 xrl.us/bmw2fq).

Ostensibly, Catullus names Cornelius as his dedicatee *nam-que tu solebas / meas esse aliquid putare nugas* <because *you* were wont to reckon my "nothings" to be *some*things> (1:3-4). But, as is often the case with Catullus, there may be more beneath the surface of the papyrus.

As with Vergil – and Catullus's fellow New Poets Valerius Cato, Gaius Cinna ("Cinna the Poet"), Furius Bibaculus, and Ticidas – Cornelius Nepos is a Transpadane, *ie,* an Italian from north of the River Po. He is likely 10 to 15 years older than Clodia, and a full generation older than Catullus. Among Cornelius's works is a world history, *Chronica* (now lost), which Catullus joshingly characterizes as *omne aevum tribus explicare cartis* <a three-volume revelation of *all* of *everything*> (1:6).

Marcello Gigante suggests (Wiseman 1979, p. 171): *in un certo senso, il poeta saluta in Cornelio uno storico neoterico* <in a certain sense, the poet salutes Cornelius as a 'New Historian'>.

Green (2005, pp. 212, 285) brings this insight into sharp focus:

> Cornelius Nepos – learned, concise, painstaking, innovative – has been described (Tatum 1997, 485) as Catullus's 'ideal reader' ..... He was an advocate, **perhaps even a patron**, of the young Neoterics. [Emphasis added.]

(Rex Stern summarizes the broad spectrum of scholarly opinion on the aptness of Nepos in this role xrl.us/bmwqb8.)

If it is Cornelius Nepos who is one of Clodia's premarital paramours, Catullus may have met Clodia through Cornelius (perhaps when the older man's affair with her is already long past). Further, Cornelius may have encouraged the interest of *both* in the New Poetry.

It might be a private joke in 1:4 that it is Clodia who has dismissed Catullus's poems as *nugas* <nothings>.

"[T]o set forth the whole history of the world in three volumes" (Francis Warre Cornish xrl.us/bmw3xo) is a typical reading of Catullus's allusion in 1:6 to Cornelius's *Chronica*. But, the more literal rendering, "a three-volume revelation of *all* of *everything*" (an otherwise inexplicable caricature in a context in which praise untinged with sarcasm would be expected), could be a 'winking' reference to Cornelius as the source of the gossip about Clodia's Brescian past (including with Cornelius himself).

Copley (1957, p. vii) asserts, "The Cornelius of two poems [he surely is referring to 1 and 102, not 67] is almost certainly Cornelius Nepos..." In contrast, regarding the Cornelius of 102 (who has a secret), Green (2005, p. 266) allows that he "*may* be Cornelius Nepos, but this is quite uncertain". [Emphasis in original.] However, if the Cornelius of 67:35-6, also, is Cornelius Nepos, then it is somewhat less uncertain that all three references are to the same Cornelius, because the general nature of this secret would be apparent in 67, as would be Catullus's extra-literary indebtedness to his dedicatee of song-poem 1.

The timeframe of Cornelius's concern that his revelations be kept confidential would most make sense at or near the beginning of Catullus's acquaintance with Clodia – while Celer is still alive and able to exact retribution. *Carmen* 67 is surely written post *magnas lites* (*Pro Caelio*) – when discretion regarding Clodia's reputation is moot.

Thus, *Carmina* 1 and 102 would form a type of overarching 'ring', with 67 as its epicenter (cf. n. 89 below).

Appendix F: *Lovely Lesbia, Meter Maid*

There remains an as-yet unaddressed paradigm that some scholars believe makes less than likely the identification of Catullus's Lesbia as Cicero's Clodia Metelli: The proposition that variations in the meter of the first two syllables of Catullus's hendecasyllables (11-syllable lines) throughout the *Passer* (the first 60 poems of the collection) establishes, in Wiseman's phrase, "chronological problems" (cf. p. 86 above) for this identification. He speculates instead that Lesbia is the sister of Clodia Metelli who was once married to Lucullus. Green (2005, p. 6), citing Mulroy, deftly disposes of this notion via an example (discussed below), which clearly contradicts Wiseman's alternative chronology.

However, in Green's reading of *Carmen* 67, "Neither the wife, nor her earlier husband and father-in-law, nor the rufous stranger are named, or really need to be" (cf. p. 45 above). By contrast, the entirety of the present volume stands or falls on my 3½-word summary of song-poem 67 on page 2 above: "It's about Clodia [Metelli]", and therefore Wiseman's arguments will receive greater attention here.

In 1957 Marcello Zicàri notes variations in the length of the first two syllables in a number of the lines of Catullus's hendecasyllablic verses. The vast majority begin with two long syllables (spondees). But, there are some that begin with a long and then a short syllable (trochees); and others that begin with a short, followed by a long syllable (iambs). In 1969 Otto Skutsch elaborates, demonstrating that the great preponderance of these variant beginning-two syllables occurs in the *second* half of the *Passer*.

Hence, some critics have drawn the inference that the first half of the *Passer* chronologically precedes the second, thus evincing authorial, or subsequent editorial, intent in the arrangement. However, this view does not prevail because, in Skinner's pithy phrasing (2007, p. 41), "Chronological arrangement has been ruled out ever since critics stopped regarding Catullus' work as a kind of poetic blog."

Yet, from these modest observations Wiseman (1974, pp. 108-

10), with seeming mathematical precision, dates the beginning of Lesbia's adulterous relationship with Catullus to *after Pro Caelio* (April 56 BCE). Since Clodia Metelli apparently is husbandless in 56 BCE (else *Pro Caelio* would have mentioned him), Catullus's adulterous affair more likely is with one of her younger sisters, who thus is the "Clodia" Apuleius identifies as Lesbia some two centuries later.

As always, Wiseman makes a case that is both learned and subtle, and hence well worth examining, and responding to. Wiseman asserts (p. 108):

> The identification of Lesbia is not vitally important itself

This *might* be so if Lesbia were *not* Clodia Metelli. But, if she *is* Clodia Metelli, then given how greatly *Pro Caelio* thereby illuminates Catullus's Lesbia, particularly in relation to Caelius Rufus, how could the identification of Lesbia not be important?

> ... but with it is involved the chronology of Catullus' life and work. Circular arguments can only be avoided if we keep the two arguments separate, and the nature of the evidence makes it (I think) essential to have the identification depend upon the chronology, and not *vice versa*.

But note, there are *two* relevant chronologies: that of the *subject matter* of the song-poems, and that of the *time* when they are written. Necessarily, the song-poems are written after the events they describe, but not necessarily *in the order* that these events have occurred. For example, though song-poem 11 (*see* p. 75 above) is, indeed, likely to have been written when the affair has come to an end, it is possible that Catullus's song-poem(s) 68A and 68B about a rendezvous with Lesbia at the home of Allius/Manlius, though having occurred early in the affair, might have been written *after* 11 is written – at a time when Catullus, perhaps quite ill, reflects upon his long friendship with Manlius, his beloved brother's premature passing (*see Carmen* 101 xrl.us/bncs2h), his own mortality, the 'death' of the hopes he once held for happiness with Lesbia, and that notwithstanding all, he still cannot stop idealizing her *venustus* <Venus-like essence, in every sense>.

Hence, even a *foolproof* methodology for dating when the 'Lesbia poems' are *written*, nonetheless – absent internal references to known historical events – may tell us very little, if anything at all, about the dating of their *subject matter*.

> There are real indications – the dateable poems – to help us with the chronology, and only illusory ones to help us with the identification. Naturally, some of the undated poems *may* be earlier (or indeed later) than the years 56-54 to which the dated ones all belong, but to put them earlier just on the strength of the Clodia Metelli hypothesis is to put far too much weight on apparent "plausibility". We need solid reasons to suppose that any of the poems belong before 56. [Emphasis in the original.]

As has been shown in Appendix D, we lack "solid reasons" to suppose that either of Clodia Metelli's sisters changes her name from *Claudia* to *Clodia*, or shares Clodia Metelli's political motives for doing so. In view of Catullus's two song-poems referring to a *Caelius*, two that name a *Rufus*, two referring to a *Caecilius*, and even one to *Cicero* (all names ineluctably associated with *Clodia Metelli* in the mind of every Roman contemporary of Catullus), what this reader finds "illusory" are the excuses conjured by a pride of classical philology's lions for their ignoring the *plain meaning* of Catullus's text – in favor of the *idée fixe de jour*.

> as Maas observed, if Catullus had been the lover of such a very political lady as Clodia Metelli since 60 B.C. or before, one might expect political allusions to appear in the poems before 56.

Other than his heated posturings (typical of those who have never themselves shouldered the burdens of elective office) about the Triumvirs Caesar and Pompey (and Caesar's chief engineer, Mamurra), Catullus's sole interest in politics seems to have been hoping to share in political spoils as an aid to Memmius during the latter's 57 BCE term as a senior official in Bithynia (now in north-central Turkey). In the event, Catullus leaves no richer (*Carmen* 10), but feels he has been orally sodomized, in the prostrate position, by Memmius (psychologically? physically? financially? *all* three? *See Carmen* 28 xrl.us/bm3o2p).

For her part, Clodia's role in politics, whatever its breadth and depth, necessarily takes place behind the scenes, because women are excluded from a public role in ancient Roman politics. She likely has some degree of influence with her husband, Celer, while he is still alive, and she is at her brother Clodius's side during his raucous oratorical confrontation with Pompey two months before the trial of Caelius (Cicero, *Quintus frater* 2.3 xrl.us/biiveq). She is certainly a source of political intelligence for Cicero and, as noted (p. 34 above), Cicero chooses her as an intermediary in his (at the time unsuccessful) attempt to repair his relationship with her brother-in-law Metellus Nepos.

However, such is not the stuff of lyric poetry. Lesbia is not Catullus's Atticus, but rather his Sappho – a source of erotic energy and poetic inspiration. Catullus is a keen observer and critic of manners and morals, not a policy wonk.

> Two of the Lesbia poems are dateable: poem 36, which implies a reconciliation of some kind, belongs after (perhaps some time after) Catullus' return from Bithynia in 56 …

Green (2005, p. 6) comments:

> Wiseman would like to down-date Catullus's relationship with Lesbia to [56-54 BCE], which would mean discarding the identification of Lesbia as Clodia Metelli. I suspect this to be one of the theory's main attractions. But as Mulroy has demonstrated (2002, xiv-xvii), Wiseman's claim that 36 (datable to a point after Catullus's return from Bithynia in 56) proves his affair to have begun only in that year doesn't make sense. If "Lesbia" is making a vow in gratitude for Catullus's safe return from abroad, the clear implication is that the relationship had indeed begun *before* his departure. [Emphasis in original.]

Wiseman then identifies 10 of the 60 *Passer* song-poems as being either explicitly or implicitly "Lesbia poems". After presenting in prose how these hendecasyllabic variations would suggest a chronological ordering for each of the 10, he provides the following table:

Carmen	Number of Variant Hendecasyllables	Number of Lines of Entire Song-poem
2	1	10
3	1 or 2	18
13	0	14
43	0	8
5	0	13
7	1 or 2	12
36	5	20
40	4	8
38	4	8
58	1	5

It is not unusual for an innovative artist to begin using a new technique in a consistent manner, and later varying this technique. Catullus, along with Calvus (*see Carmen* 50 xrl.us/bm 3foc), are the New Poets who popularize hendecasyllablic verse in Latin poetry (Green 2005, p. 32).

Hence, variance from the standard long-long beginning of a hendecasyllable is a facially plausible metric for hypothesizing an order in which the first 60 song-poems of the Catullan collection are *written*.

From the above data Wiseman surmises:

> Since the developed technique, of which there is no sign in the immediately post-Bithynia poems, is beginning to appear in some of the early poems to Lesbia, I conclude that there is good reason not to put the beginning of the affair before 56 B.C.

But, as discussed (pp. 133-34 above), a plausible hypothesis for when the song-poems of the *Passer* are written is not necessarily a reliable metric for the determination of when the events described therein have occurred.

Wiseman then elaborates on logical corollaries to his chronology:

Catullus' liaison with one of the three Clodiae [*sic*], therefore, evidently had its idyllic beginning some time soon after the summer of 56 B.C., and had passed through the stages of doubt, reconciliation, resignation and jealous fury probably by the winter of 55-4, to end with the harsh message of farewell in poem 11. A "long love" it must have seemed to the man who had gone through it (76.13), even if it lasted little more than a year.

The above scenario is *conceivable*. But, do the words "must have ..." accurately reflect its likelihood? (It might be asked, as an aside: If Catullus were *really* 'over' Lesbia, why does he write, in *Sapphic* stanza, the 24-line *Carmen* 11?)

If we could measure the amount of self-deception of which Catullus was capable, we might even be able to rule out one of the three sisters. Could the innocent hopes of mutual fidelity with which he started out really have been possible with Clodia Metelli in 56 B.C., only a few months after the devastating publicity given to her way of life by Cicero and Caelius at the latter's trial? Perhaps they could. But the dates must make her the least likely of the Clodiae to have been Catullus' mistress.

Note that, all other things being equal, this line of reasoning also would apply to Wiseman's favored candidate for Lesbia, Clodia's likewise adulterous and incestuous sister Claudia Luculli – subsequent to the testimony about *her* in their brother Clodius's trial for *Incestus*.

However, not all other things are equal here: An affair with Clodia Metelli likely would have begun when Catullus is still in his early 20s. By 56 BCE Catullus, just having returned from Bithynia, is surely more worldly-wise than he was when Clodia Metelli is still married to Celer.

Green (2005, p. 3) observes regarding Catullus's early death:

Bearing in mind the brief lives of both brothers, the hacking cough to which Catullus seems to have been a martyr (44), his references – not necessarily or exclusively metaphorical – to a chronic and unpleasant malaise (76, ?38), his febrile intensity (50), and, not least, his intense and debilitating erotic preoccupations, it seems distinctly possible that tuberculosis (one of the great silent scourges of antiquity) ran in the family and was the cause of his death. [If so, this is another of the benchmarks Catullus sets for future Romantic poets.]

If Green's conjecture is correct, by 56 BCE Catullus already has had intimations of the final pyre. Even if not, it is hard to believe likely that post-*Bithynia* Catullus is struck deaf, dumb, and blind merely by being in Lesbia's presence (Carmen 51 xrl.us/bmfir4), whoever she may be.

As noted (p. 47 above), Clodia Metelli is the only one of the three sisters who is *known* to be married at a time when Catullus is likely old enough to enter into a serious romance with a married woman. Wiseman (1974, p. 111) addresses the matter thus:

> Whichever one of the three it was, she was married. She came to Catullus at Allius' house from her husband's bed (68:146); she abused him before her husband, which he took as proof of her love (83). It was not Metellus Celer (died in 59), nor Marcius Rex [the third sister's husband] (died in 61), nor L. Lucullus (divorced in 66), but Lesbia's second husband. Remarriage was normal among Roman noblewomen, and it is likely enough that all three of the sisters married again.[33]
>
> 33 Clodia Metelli had not yet done so in April 56 – another reason why she is the least likely of the three.

If it is "likely enough" that all three sisters remarry, yet Clodia Metelli has not done so by 56 BCE, why is not likely enough that neither have either of her sisters?

Note that, once again, the unnecessary complication of an unattested second husband has been introduced – in order to solve a 'problem' that arises only from a refusal to accept the plain meaning of the text. This results in more, not fewer, 'riddles', *eg*, if Lesbia is not Clodia Metelli, who is Lesbia's *cuckold?* If *Caelius* and *Rufus* do not refer to Caelius Rufus, to whom *do* these names refer? If Caelius Rufus does not have a Veronese past, who is the *Caelius* who *does?* If *Pro Caelio* were not the subtext of the thank-you note to Cicero, what *was?* And, so forth.

Endnotes

1. Wiseman (1987, p. 1). My (admittedly nonprofessional) view is that Wiseman is the most learned living classicist. *See* also *The Harry Potter* connection: xrl. us/bikugk.

2. Perlovsky (3.3):

> In humans, primates, and some other social animals, there are neurons that are excited when manipulating objects, and the same neurons are excited, when observing ano-ther animal making similar gestures. MNS [Mirror Neuron System] involves areas of brain near Broca area, where today resides human language ability.

3. The French philologist Adrianus Turnebus (1512 – 1565) suggests that *Caecilius* in 67:9 is a reference to Celer. Of Tur-nebus's speculation, Pierre Bayle, *et al*, remark (pp. 545-46):

> [Turnebus] imagined that Catullus spoke of our Metellus Celer in [*Carmen* 67] ..... Scaliger [1540 – 1609, Turne-bus's one-time pupil] refutes Turnebus by two arguments: the first is that the scene of this adventure was at Vero-na, and not at Rome; the second is that it was never said that Clodia committed incest with her father [*sic*]. Cicero would not have failed to reproach her with it, if her repu-tation had ever been sullied in this article ..... These two reasons of Scaliger's are very strong ones ...

To this reader, Scaliger's two reasons are very *weak* ones. As is discussed in greater detail (p. 86 above), Wiseman, though he thinks Lesbia more likely to be one of our Clodia's sisters, cites song-poems 86 and 100 in observing: "Lesbia herself was certainly not unknown to the *provincia* [*ie*, Verona]".

Regarding Cicero's silence about her 'past' (with her father-*in-law*) during his verbal assault on Clodia's character: With choking voice and tears in his eyes while he is strongly suggesting that Clodia fatally poisoned her husband, Celer, Cicero describes the deceased Consul in the most heroic terms (*Pro Caelio* 59; *see* p. 19 above). Cicero would not risk tarnishing Celer's manly lustre by allowing that Celer was bested in the *boudoir* by his own father.

However, *Catullus* already has a history of disparaging Celer's marital manhood (see n. 16 below). Unlike Cicero, at this juncture he has no tactical motive to be reticent about gleefully publicizing this extended episode in Clodia's past.

Of note: It appears that Turnebus does not expand upon his bare conjecture. Hugh Munro (p. 160) quotes him summarizing song-poem 67 thus: *aeque ac folium Sibyllae obscurum et tenebricosum* <loosely: and yet, equally clouded with obscurity as a page from the Sibylline Books>.

4.   By inference from:

> *haec tota fabella veteris et plurimarum fabularum poetriae quam est sine argumento quam nullum invenire exitum potest* (*Pro Caelio* 64 xrl.us/bkowsk)

> Hence, this whole drama and the plethora of a poetess's confabulations should be given a *thumbs-down* by you [Jurists] – as it is *without plausibility*, as it is possible to find *no exit!*

Austin, p. 149: "Cicero's speech and the fragments of Caelius' own defence point to the existence of a coterie of Clodia's Young Men ... " [Capitalization in the original.]

Skinner (2010, p. 79): "[Clodia] must have been born shortly after the turn of the century, in approximately 98 [BCE]."

Pulchra is the source of the English word "pulchritude".

5. Green (2005, p. 11):

> It was their older contemporary Cicero who described this group of young poets as 'Neoterics' (οἱ νεώτεροι, 'the younger ones' or 'the innovators'), or 'the new poets' (*poetae noui*). He did not mean the label as a compliment (*Orat.* 161 [xrl.us/bmd7dk]; *Tusc.* 3.45 [xrl.us/bmd7dp]) ...

However Cicero, like Catullus, is not without a sense of irony and a fondness for wordplay. His family being of neither noble nor senatorial rank, Cicero's own social status is that of *novo homo* <newcomer>. It is possible that he sees a parallel of a sort to his own status – in the discontinuity between the New Poets and the traditional poetic elite – and thus is paying them a perhaps grudging, but still sincere, compliment.

Catulus (with *one* "l") in Latin means "puppy"; his dates are likely *c.* 84 – *c.* 54 BCE (*see* Green 2005, pp. 1-2).

The identification of Catullus's Lesbia as the Clodia Metelli of Cicero's *Pro Caelio* is discussed at pp. 46-78 and Appendices D and F above.

6. Wiseman (1987, p. 65): "[Caelius Rufus] was tall, strikingly handsome, a dandy in his dress and with a taste for extravagant social life." "Rusty" approximates *Rufus* as a contemporary *cognomen* <nickname>.

The historian Pliny sets Caelius's date of birth as May 28, 82 BCE (*Naturalis Historia* 7:165 xrl.us/bmdfap). Since this date implies Caelius was elected to public offices when younger than the statutory minimum, some scholars assume an earlier date of birth.

Skinner (2010, pp. 102-03), for example, sets Caelius's birth five years earlier in order to coincide with these age limits. However in *Pro Caelio*, by my count, Cicero – in order to exculpate Caelius of charges of sexual wantonness – uses variants of the words *adulescens* <young man>, *aetas* <time of life>, and *iuventus* <youth>, respectively, 39, 25, and 8 times, totaling 72 references to Caelius's youth. Were Caelius then age 31 – or 32 (Wiseman 1987, p. 62) – more than 70 references to his 'youth' would seem counterproductive.

Austin (pp. 144-45) observes that in *Pro Caelio* 9-11 xrl.us/bikutx, Cicero insists he was a completely successful guardian of Caelius's virtue from ages 16-19 (according to Pliny's date). To claim instead that Caelius, of all people, was still a virgin at age 24 or 25 would get Cicero laughed out of court. Austin concludes: "Pliny's date exactly fits Cicero's evidence."

7. Of the name *Cicero*, Plutarch relates:

> For 'cicer' is the Latin name for chick-pea, and this ancestor of Cicero, as it would seem, had a faint dent in the end of his nose like the cleft of a chick-pea, from which he acquired his surname. (Perrin, *Plutarch: Parallel Lives – Cicero* 1.2 xrl.us/bmkik9)

8. Shackleton Bailey (pp. 15-16), writing of this period:

With the expansion of the empire the machinery of government had become hopelessly inadequate; wars were mismanaged, provinces oppressed and exploited, corruption was rampant in polling-booth and court-room.

9. Skinner (2010, p. 23) citing Suetonius, *De Vita Caesarum – Tiberius* 1.2 xrl.us/bmdh3c.

10. Martial, *Epigrammata* 14:195 xrl.us/bmebuk:

tantum magna suo debet verona catullo quantum parva suo mantua vergilio

Mighty Verona is as indebted to her Catullus as mitey Mantua to her Vergil.

David S Levene ("The Late Republican/Triumviral Period: 90-40 BC", pp. 31, 33; in Stephen Harrison, ed.):

Although it is a period from which a substantial amount of literature in a wide variety of genres survives, more than 75 per cent of that literature was written by a single man: Marcus Tullius Cicero ..... The Romans themselves of the following generations, who could read much that now is lost, when they looked back to the literature of the last years of the Republic, saw it above all as 'the age of Cicero'.

11. *See* Skinner (1983 and 2010) generally.

12. *See*, for example: "Strauss-Kahn Charged in Prostitution Case", *New York Times*, Mar 28, 2012 xrl.us/bmzpv3.

13. Cp. The Shields, "You Cheated, You Lied" xrl.us/bmdbp7.

14. Cp. Connie Francis, "Who's Sorry Now" bit.ly/p47me.

15. *See* "Isle of Lesbos" xrl.us/bmeo6a.

16. *Carmen* 17:26 xrl.us/bmfb3x: *mula* <mule>. *Carmen* 67:20-22:

non illam vir prior attigerit languidior tenera cui pendens sicula beta nunquam se mediam sustulit ad tunicam

Not that [Celer] *could have* touched her beforehand / he who, *little* dagger drooping limper than the letter *lambda*, never got it up to half-mast!

Carmen 83:3 xrl.us/bmh5tj: *mule* <mule>.

"Celer", the source of our "accelerate", is the *cognomen* <nickname> of Clodia's husband. "Swifty" approximates its meaning in English. From the point of view of military colleagues, the nickname "Swifty" likely connotes a commander's dashing derring-do. However, from his pleasure-loving wife's point of view, it may connote a source of marital disappointment – no less so for an artistically gifted woman who inspires in her most impassioned paramour the term of endearment "Lesbia".

17. *See* Appendix A.

18. Austin (p. 149):

> ... Caelius was the younger and had more staying power than Catullus; Clodia may have found him more fun; he was cynical and calculating and cool ...

The identification of the Caelius of *Carmen* 100 with the Caelius Rufus of *Pro Caelio* is discussed on pp. 47-8, 82-3, 86 above.

19. In light of Catullus's allusiveness (a cornerstone of the New Poets' program), it is difficult for this reader to believe that the parallels between the two poetesses, Sappho and Clodia/"Lesbia", are exclusively literary.

Ellen Greene ("Catullus and Sappho", pp. 132, 133, in Skinner, ed., 2007):

> Owing mainly to the homoerotic features of her verse and her powerful expressions of erotic desire, Sappho's literary reputation in Rome is often associated with sexual impropriety and degeneracy ..... While we certainly cannot equate the figure of Lesbia with Sappho, it is nonetheless fair to say that allusions to Lesbia in Catullus' poetry evoke in varying ways the poetics and persona of Sappho.

For a less expansive reading of the pseudonym "Lesbia", *see* Wiseman 1987, pp. 130-36, especially 135.

20. Julia Dyson (Hejduk) ("The Lesbia Poems", Skinner, ed., 2007, pp. 266-67):

> With poem 68, considered by many "the most extraordi-

nary poem in Latin" (Lyne 1980: 52; Feeney 1992: 33), Catullus completely changes the terms in which Lesbia is conceived ..... [*Domina*] refers solely to a woman in control of slaves. With this line, Catullus plants the seed for a theme to blossom fully only in his poetic successors, the *servitium amoris* or "slavery of love," which portrays the poet as the "slave" of a "mistress" in control of his heart.

Cp. Sam Cooke: "Bring It on Home to Me" bit.ly/83jxj7.

Regarding Clodia's relationships with certain of her *literal* slaves, the scandalized Cicero roars:

> *at quibus servis refert ... eisne quos intellegebat non communi condicione servitutis uti sed licentius liberius familiariusque cum domina vivere* (*Pro Caelio* 57 xrl.us/bkihf6)

> And, 'slaves' to *what!?* .... Weren't they for that which is not understood as the *common* conduct of servitude, but instead to live quite licentiously, quite lasciviously, and quite intimately with the *Domina?!*

For an extended treatment of high-born Roman women maintaining their independence from a husband of their own class by engaging in intimate relations with a slave (including in some cases a eunuch), and on occasion marrying a slave – as well as the alarmed Roman patriarchy's apparently limited success in suppressing the practice, *see* Evans-Grubbs generally.

21. Mrs Billie McClarty, 2008; Elvis Presley Birthplace, Tupelo, Mississippi. Personal communication explaining why Jesse's remains are not interred at Graceland in Memphis, Tennessee, with the rest of his immediate family.

22. *See* p. 67 above; *see* also Charlotte Higgins, "Catullus Still Shocks 2,000 Years On". *The Guardian*, November 24, 2009 xrl.us/bmev48.

23. Sammy Davis, Jr xrl.us/bmdijn at 1:58.

It is not implausible that Catullus and Elvis have a partially shared ethnic heritage. Herbert Jennings Rose (p. 542) notes:

> [Catullus] was no Roman by birth, for Verona is in Cisalpine Gaul. In that region Keltic blood is not an impossibi-

lity [indeed, it is a likelihood]; and when was there a Kelt who had not some feeling for language?

Though of mixed heritage (in part Cherokee, with a Jewish great grandmother via unbroken matrilineal descent), Elvis is of primarily Keltic ancestry, as is obvious from his name.

24. Greene (p. 132):

> The world of feminine desire and poetic imagination evoked in Sappho's poetry is an integral feature of Catullan love lyric, and, more specifically, serves as a vehicle for Catullus' implicit critique of aspects of Roman social and aesthetic values.

Cp. Sappho 31, "To a Woman" xrl.us/bmfis7; Catullus, *Carmen* 51 xrl.us/bmfptf; Elvis, "All Shook Up" bit.ly/h1pr2T.

25. Sappho 31, audio: bit.ly/pLqttW; Catullus, *Carmen* 5, audio: bit.ly/98WRBI; Elvis, "Love Me Tender" bit.ly/nHgxHY.

26. The Praetutii: xrl.us/bmfkd7. *Pro Caelio* 5 xrl.us/bikujo. *See* Austin (pp. 146-47) on the uncertainty of the manuscript.

27. Catullus, *Carmen* 100. (*See* pp. 47-48, 82-83, 86 above.)

28. "Cicero was a friend of Clodius, and in the affair of Catiline had found him a most eager co-worker and guardian of his person ..." (Perrin, *Plutarch: Parallel Lives – Cicero* 29.1 xrl.us/bmbsxe).

29. Cicero, *Atticus* 1.16.10 xrl.us/bmdpko.

30. Skinner (2010, p. 64): "As the wife of a former praetor and current proconsul of Cisalpine Gaul, Clodia would surely have been present ..."

How else could a mere 'slave-girl' gain admittance to Rome's most exclusive all-women event – unless Clodius were posing as a slave-girl of Clodia?

31. Shackleton Bailey (p. 42):

> Even the name of the mysterious divinity whom [male] Romans called 'the Good Goddess' and [male] Greeks 'the Women's Goddess' was not for masculine ears; and only women might be present at her secret ritual held every

year in Rome at the beginning of December.

32. Perrin, *Plutarch: Parallel Lives – Cicero* 28.2 ff. xrl.us/b mdmod. Tatum (pp. 66, 67):

> Clodius' intrusion brought the service to a halt. Indeed, the sources report that pandemonium broke out when his deep voice signaled his gender ..... The scandal could not but have aroused the Romans' throttling censoriousness.

33. *rem p conservassem* <savior of the Republic> (Cicero, *Familiares* 5.2.7 xrl.us/bmdft9) is a phrase characteristic of Cicero's self-assessment.

34. Cicero, *Atticus* 1.16.5 xrl.us/bmfrya:

> *biduo per unum servum et eum ex ludo gladiatorio confecit totum negotium arcessivit ad se promisit intercessit dedit iam vero o di boni rem perditam etiam noctes certarum mulierum atque adulescentulorum nobilium introductiones non nullis iudicibus pro mercedis cumulo fuerunt*

> Within two days, [Calvus the Orator/New Poet or Crassus the Triumvir (referent uncertain)] completed the whole deal via a single *slave*. (And he from the *gladiatorial* ring!) He *convened*. He *promised*. He *guaranteed*. He *paid*.

> *That's* not all. (Oh, Good God, the decadence!) Furthermore, as an added 'bonus', for not a few Jurists there were 'overnights' with certain 'ladies', and also the 'introductions' of certain boys of the nobility!

35. Tatum (pp. 103, 04):

> The first months of Caesar's consulship proved utterly shocking .... Cicero, who shared the senate's alarm and indignation over Caesar's methods, became anxious over his own position as well .... [T]hanks to its own extreme methods, the [Triumvirate] had to anticipate a backlash once its opposition became galvanized (a process hastened by their enormities) and once that opposition found an opportunity to strike back. One such moment seemed to come at the trial of C. Antonius, Cicero's unsavory fellow consul in 63 .... His defense of Antonius took the shape of a contumacious diatribe, exposing the threat to the

republic by the triumvirs' violence and in particular de-
nouncing Caesar virulently.

36. Skinner (2010, p. 104):

Was it pure coincidence, then, that Caelius found lodging
in a complex owned by Clodia's brother? Since the district was so exclusive, a property owner or his manager
would doubtless screen prospective tenants closely; perhaps Caelius qualified as a desirable occupant because
he and Clodius were already well acquainted.

37. *Carmina* 58, 69, 77, and 100, *inter alia*.

38. Cicero, *Pro Caelio* 60 xrl.us/bkjhqe:

*qui consul incipientem furere atque tonantem sua
se manu interfecturum audiente senatu dixerit*

The Consul [Celer] who from the beginning, with the Senate listening, spoke of doing-in with his own hand the
sound and fury [of Clodius]!

39. Wiseman (1987, p. 64). *See* also, Tatum, pp. 104, 105:

Within only a few hours of Cicero's speech, the triumvirs
arranged for Clodius to become a plebeian ..... Clodius
did not become Fonteius's heir, but instead continued
using his old name and to maintain Claudian *sacra*
[<familial sacred objects>].

40. Shackleton Bailey (p. 62):

When Piso, who was related to Cicero's son-in-law, was
approached (Gabinius being obviously hopeless), he de-
clined to interfere; the best thing, he suggested, was for
Cicero to leave Rome. Personal appeals by Cicero, both to
Piso and Pompey were equally unproductive. Years later
he wrote to Atticus that when he lay at Pompey's feet,
Pompey did not even ask him to get up, but merely said
he could do nothing against Caesar's wishes. Despite all
warnings, this final rejection came as a shock .... And
those to whom he turned for advice were nearly all of
Piso's opinion: he had better retire from Rome.

41. By inference from Cicero, *Pro Caelio* 52 xrl.us/bidifo:

tune aurum ex armario tuo promere ausa es tune venerem illam tuam spoliare ornamentis spoliatricem ceterorum

Didn't you audaciously produce the gold from your 'trophy closet'? *Didn't* you strip, from your well-known statue of Venus, jewelry stripped from *others?*

Susan Treggiari (pp. 60-61):

[Terentia and Tullia] put on their black clothes and left their hair dishevelled in order to show themselves outside in the classic form of protest, and they visited the houses of others in order to work for Cicero's return.

After Cicero left, the Council of the Plebs passed both Clodius' bills. Terentia and Tullia now knew where they stood. It must, even so, have been a terrible shock when Clodius' supporters came to burn down the Palatine house and loot the contents. The villas at Tusculum and Formiae were also plundered and burned, and the rest of the property put on sale.

.....Furniture and silverware were, naturally, pilfered. [Terentia] and her household escaped, perhaps warned before the mob arrived, and she took refuge (probably with her half-sister Fabia) in the house of the Vestal Virgins about five minutes' walk away.

42. *See* Appendix B.

43. Cp. Marlene Dietrich and Charles Laughton, *Witness for the Prosecution* bit.ly/utqOEG.

44. Hugh Chisholm, ed., p. 150 xrl.us/bmhhzg.

45. Cicero, *Quintus Frater* 2.3.3 xrl.us/bmfp4n.

46. The name of the Egyptian dictator here at issue is Ptolemy ("the Flautist") Auletes. A stable resolution of this particular 'Arab Spring' will not come until the arrival in Alexandria of Caesar in 48 BCE, where his hosts seek to please him by presenting him with the severed head of his rival for power, Pompey the Great. (Caesar is not amused.)

It is there that Caesar meets, and installs on the Egyptian throne, the by-then deceased Ptolemy's 21-year-old daughter, the famed Cleopatra.

Some recent commentators assert that Cleopatra is not as glamorous as legend has it. Yet, it is undeniable that she succeeds in enchanting both Caesar and, subsequently, Mark Antony. So, surely, she is not without her charms.

Interestingly, a bare month after Caesar's assassination, Cicero, writing to Atticus (his confidant and intermediary with Clodia), mentions the two women in virtually the same breath (*Atticus* 14.8.1; 16 April 44 BCE <u>xrl.us/bmip9g</u>):

> *reginae fuga mihi non molesta est clodia quid egerit scribas ad me*

> The Queen's [Cleopatra's] flight has not been worrying me. About Clodia: Whatever she shall have done, I would that you write to me.

Skinner (2010, p. 119) suggests:

> [W]e might wonder if the question "What has Clodia done?" immediately following mention of Cleopatra's departure in the letter of April 44 refers to the fact that Cleopatra had been Clodia's guest at the famous garden estate. Perhaps her hurried leavetaking had disrupted some plans of her hostess.

47. Wiseman (1987, p. 70-71):

> Within the space were the presiding magistrate [Gnaeus Domitius Calvinus] on his tribunal, the three *decuriae* of judges on their benches (usually 25 men in each *decuria*, but there may have been more in the Caelius case, with no other courts in session), and confronting each other from opposite sides, the benches of the prosecution and defence.

48. Mojtaba Kazazi (p. 54): *actori incumbit probatio* <on the accuser lies proof> <u>xrl.us/bidjz6</u>.

49. Victoria Zdrok (p. 42):

> Results confirmed belief perseverance effect, showing that

participants were affected by previous information, even if they knew from the outset that the event to be explained was hypothetical. The Researchers concluded that when people encode presented information, they construct causal links between the to-be-ignored and the to-be-used information. This integrative coding then impairs successful discounting of invalid information.

It could be argued that belief perseverance equally applies to the traditional reading of Cicero's and Catullus's account of Clodia's character (see Wiseman 1987, p. 1). And, to some extent, that argument has merit. However, unlike a jury under pressure to render a timely verdict (or the subjects of a lab experiment), there is no time limit on evaluating the veracity of the claims of Cicero and Catullus about Clodia.

A jury may not look beyond the trial testimony and the exhibits entered into evidence. Whereas, any reader whose local library has an internet connection has access thereby to a plethora of information unavailable to a jury engaged in its deliberations.

Eventually, suggestions that contradict the evidence and/or their own internal logic are likely to be sifted out. The work herein is offered as a contribution to that process.

50. Hence, statements such as: "Cicero simply invented the relationship between Caelius and Clodia ..." (Holzberg, p. 30, citing Stroh and Kennedy) cannot withstand even minimal scrutiny.

51. Lintott, p. 432: "The speech is technically adept but above all has the feeling of a relaxed performance."

Thus, Cicero wisecracks:

> *quod quidem facerem vehementius nisi intercederent mihi inimicitiae cum istius mulieris viro fratrem volui dicere semper hic erro nunc agam modice nec longius progrediar quam me mea fides et causa ipsa coget nec enim muliebris umquam inimicitias mihi gerendas putavi praesertim cum ea quam omnes semper amicam omnium potius quam cuiusquam inimicam putaverunt (Pro Caelio 32 xrl.us/bif5ri)*

Indeed, I would assuredly be more vehement, but for the conflicts that have come between me and that woman's husband – *brother*, I meant to say! (I always err *thus*.)

Now I shall go forward in moderation; I shall advance no further than my duty and the case itself will require. For certainly, I do not believe in ever bearing enmity against a woman – *particularly* with her whom all consider always a 'friend' of *all* the men, rather than an enemy of *any*.

52. As far back as four years earlier in a letter to Atticus, the (mirthfully) apologetic Cicero displays his wit by sharing a naughty riposte he has made at the expense of Clodius and Clodia: Clodius, implicitly bragging that his current Quaestership in Sicily is far more splendid than was Cicero's 15 years earlier, approaches Cicero 'complaining' that Clodia will not employ her influence as the wife of Celer (then Consul) to afford Clodius's Sicilian guests more than *solum pedem* <only a *foot*> of space at public spectacles. Cicero puns in reply: *noli inquam de uno pede sororis queri licet etiam alterum tollas* <Don't complain – if your sister offers a *foot*, lift her *other* one too!> (*Atticus* 2.1.5 xrl.us/bifmim)

Lintott, p. 432:

> As far as we can judge from the surviving fragments, the invective against Clodius and Curio, delivered in the senate in 61 after Clodius' unexpected acquittal for sacrilege, and the consequent altercation with Clodius gave a foretaste of the pro Caelio.

53. *Pro Caelio* 68 xrl.us/bkprhx:

> *tandem aliquid invenimus quod ista mulier de suorum propinquorum fortissimorum virorum sententia atque auctoritate fecisse dicatur*

> At *last!* We come upon *something* that this woman is claimed to have done on the advice of her most valiant kindred-men! But, I desire to know what *evidence* would there be of this manumission?

54. *Pro Caelio* 6-9, 18, 20, 25-26, 29, 30, 35-50, 74, 76-77.

55. Wilde vs Queensberry xrl.us/bmiair: "[Wilde] claimed to regard the letters as works of art rather than as something to be ashamed of."

Cp. *Carmen* 16:5-6:

> *nam castum esse decet pium poetam*
> *ipsum versiculos nihil necesse est*

> It is proper for a poet to be piously pure –
> his verselets need not be.

56. Austin (p. vii) asserts: "[T]he second accusation never took shape". Wiseman (1987, p. 67, n. 72), however, cites Cicero, *Philippica* 11.11 xrl.us/bmxhsg.

Crawford (p. 143 xrl.us/bmefiq) elaborates:

> ... Cicero himself admits that Bestia was convicted at the sixth trial (Phil. 11.11 = A) for offenses committed while seeking the praetorship in 57. This trial must be the last; therefore it must be after April of 56, when the *Pro Caelio* took place. At the time of his own trial, Caelius was preparing to indict the father of L. Sempronius Atratinus, who, it has been shown, was L. Calpurnius Bestia. This indictment, the second to be attempted under the *lex Tullia de ambitu* [<law against vote-buying>] (Cic. *Pro Cael.* 16,56, 76,78), must have involved the campaign for the praetorship. It was ultimately successful; Bestia was convicted and went into exile until he was recalled by Caesar and M. Antony in 44.

Austin may mean that Caelius is not the orator who brings this subsequent prosecution, but it indeed is brought – this time successfully.

57. Wiseman 1987, p. 69: "[T]his trial would itself be a public spectacle as dramatic as anything to be seen in the theatre or the Circus."

Cp. *quo mea se molli candida diva pede | intulit* (68B:70-1 xrl.us/bmhhd2)

> There my iridescent Goddess her emollient ped conferred.

58. *Pro Caelio* – Indirect references to breakup: *nimis acerbo odio* <limitless bitter hate> (2); *ex inimica ex crudeli ... irata mulier* <from the enmity, from the cruelty ... of an angry woman> (55); *inimicitias odiumque* <enmity and odium> (75). Direct references: *iurgi petulantis* <petulant spat> (30); *magnum rursus odium video cum crudelissimo discidio exstitisse* <I see a reversal: Great hate arises from a most tempestuous parting of the ways> (31); *verbis parvam* <sarcastically: a few 'little words'> (36); *sin autem iam suberat simultas exstincta erat consuetudo discidium exstiterat* <Unless, however, dissension were already underway – discord had arisen!> (61).

59. Wiseman (1987, p. 131): "Even under the protection of her pseudonym, [Lesbia] is not named with any identifiable man except Catullus himself." More precisely, not named with any man identifiable *with certainty*.

60. Jonah Lendering xrl.us/bmcco6:

> Callimachus' contribution consisted of no less than 800 books, but almost everything is lost, including his *Pinakes*, a classification of Greek literature in 120 books. However, we can reconstruct his *Aetia* ("Causes", the origins of several religious rituals, including a famous poem on Berenice's hair tresses), *Iambic poems*, a short epic called *Hecale*, and six *Hymns* to several gods. In these works, Callimachus presents himself as a scholar who delights in surprising his reader with unexpected turns, learned literary allusions, technical refinement, and sophistication.

Queen Berenice's hair: Cp. *Carmen* 66 xrl.us/bmfcij.

61. *See* Appendix C.

62. Wiseman (1987, p. 23) cites, with regard to Clodius, orations of Cicero (among others, *Haruspicum Responsis* and *Pro Sestio*), pertinent portions of which read:

> *si cadet quod di omen obruant a viro tamen confecta videatur qui post patris mortem primam illam aetatulam suam ad scurrarum locupletium libidines detulit quorum intemperantia expleta in domesticis est germanitatis stupris volutatus* (Cic. *Har.* 42; xrl.us/bidx8w)

If [Rome] shall fall – heaven forbid – let it at least appear to have been defeated by a *man!* [Not someone] who after his father's death, at that young age first fed the appetites of the idle rich, whom having been sated, turned to domestic strumpetry with his *sister!*

sed cum scurrarum locupletium scorto cum sororis adultero cum stuprorum sacerdote (Cic. *Sest.* 39 xrl.us/bignqk)

But I had to contend with a boytoy of the idle rich, with an adulterer of his *sister*, with a 'high priest' of *strumpetry*.

Note that here Cicero sets the date of Clodius's fall from virtue as subsequent to his father's death in 76 BCE. Clodius's year of birth was likely 92 or 93 BCE (Tatum, p. 33; Skinner 2010, p. 52), implying he was 15 or 16 when his father died.

Contemporary political invective, including charges of sexual impropriety, are not notably lacking in accuracy. I find no reason, *a priori*, to infer inaccuracy from their frequency in ancient Rome.

63. Tatum (p. 35); Wiseman (1987, p. 18, n. 4).

64. Yet, perhaps not. Giangrande (pp. 93-98) provides an exacting five-page explanation of what the husband's impaired sexual function will allow him to do, and what it will not. Included in his explanation are two Roman Deities of whose existence this reader has not been previously aware: *Deus Pertundus* <the Penetration God> (pp. 95 n. 35; 96; 97-98; 101), and *Dea Pertunda* <the Penetration Goddess> (p. 97).

65. The innuendo as to the paternity of Clodia's daughter, Metella, is apparent. Whoever may have been her biological father, Metella "inherited her mother's reputation" (Green 2005, p. 283; *see* also Wiseman 1974, pp. 188-90). While married to Lentulus Spinther, Metella conducts an open affair with a friend of Caelius, Publius Dolabella, the political radical and dissolute playboy husband of Cicero's daughter, Tullia (Skinner 2010, pp. 6, 90-95).

As a consequence, Tullia divorces Dolabella while still pregnant with their child, who dies in childbirth. Tullia herself dies about a month later (February 45 BCE), leaving Cicero grief-stricken, as he relates in reply to a letter of condolence:

*amissis ornamentis iis quae ipse commemoras quaeque
eram maximis laboribus adeptus unum manebat illud sola-
cium quod ereptum est (Familiares* 4.6.2 <u>xrl.us/bmiat3</u>)

Having been stripped of the trappings of office (about
which you yourself comment) and whatever had been
attained by the hardest labor, there remained that one
solace – *which has been ripped away.*

Tullia's death is the occasion for Cicero to request that Atticus inquire of Clodia if she would sell her riverfront gardens
(apparently the same pleasure-gardens in which she and
Caelius once dallied), in order that Cicero might create there
a sanctuary in memory of Tullia. It seems that nothing came
of this plan, but it can be inferred from Cicero's letters that
Clodia did not remarry, and that she was able to convey her
property on her own behalf, without the intermediation of a
male member of her family.

65.1 Cp. *Carmen* 68B:135-40:

*quae tamen etsi uno non est contenta catullo
rara verecundae furta feremus erae
ne nimium simus stultorum more molesti
saepe etiam iuno maxima caelicolum
coniugis in culpa flagrantem contudit iram
noscens omnivoli plurima furta iovis*

And, though she is not content with just *one* 'Catullus',
we endure the rare affair of a modest Mistress
lest we become too much bother, like a silly simian sap.
Often even Juno, Queen of Heaven,
swallowed burning rage, cognizant of the conjugal cul-
pability
of furtively polyamorous Jove.

Note that, consistent with his consciousness of their role-
reversal, Catullus here compares himself not with a cuckolded man, but rather with a woman whose man cheats on her.

Note further that his metaphor for other men in Clodia's life,
etsi uno non ... catullo <not just *one* 'Catullus'> implies Clodia's other lovers are also from her circle of New Poets. (Cf.
Clodia's Young Men, n. 4 above.)

66. "[M]addeningly confusing": Skinner (2003, p. 46); "riddle": Copley (dismissively; 1949, p. 245); "enigma": Lawrence Richardson (p. 423).

67. *Carmen* 58:1 xrl.us/bmfbrv; cp. *Notre Dame* and *Cosa Nostra*.

68. Whatever may be the deficiencies in my reading of song-poem 67, it implies that Catullus has succeeded swimmingly.

69. Apuleius lived *c.* 125 CE – *c.* 180 CE, and was a prolific writer on, *inter alia*, cultic subjects.

70. Patsy Cline, "Tennessee Waltz" xrl.us/bmcgvi.

71. Conway Twitty, "It's Only Make Believe" bit.ly/r0a2cV.

72. Marilyn Monroe, "Diamonds Are a Girl's Best Friend" bit.ly/nR69y.

73. Holzberg (p. 29):

> Not that the novel-like tale of Catullus's life which emerges from such interpretations – young poet from the provinces goes to the big city, falls into the clutches of a dissolute married older woman, is overwhelmed by his intense, but unrequited love for her, dies an untimely death – no longer haunts us. It does so in several very recent studies, in fact, such as the books of T. P. Wiseman (1985), Charles Martin (1992), and D. F. S. Thomson's lengthy 1997 commentary. On the whole, however, the 'Catullus Romance' is at least gradually being faded out of Catullan studies now. And yet even scholars who apply the most modern of literary theories to Catullus' work continue to read Lesbia as pseudonym for Clodia, and will insist on identifying the *puella* [<Mistress>] with whom Catullus's *persona* [<identity as entertainer>] is in love as a real, live person, and on including this historical *puella* in their interpretations.

> ..... The parallels drawn [between Lesbia and Clodia] are not between poetry and reality, but between poetry and another form of fiction, since the Clodia in Cicero's *Pro Caelio* is certainly as much a product of 'womanufacture' as Catullus's Lesbia.

Perhaps this "insistence" on the part of even scholars employing the most modern of critical methods is due to the difficulty in removing the Romance from Romans – *eg*, Clodia/Lesbia, Catullus, and Caelius.

74. Holzberg (p. 30, citing Stroh): "[T]he word *vir* [<usually: husband or man>] can also mean the partner of a hetaera ..."

75. Holzberg (*ibid*): "Cicero simply invented the relationship between Caelius and Clodia to suit his own rhetorical purposes."

76. Suetonius indicates that Catullus's poems permanently damage Caesar's reputation (*see Carmina* 29 xrl.us/bmrbha and 57). By way of demonstrating Caesar's magnanimity toward even opponents who have done him lasting harm, Suetonius cites a 'wine summit' attended by the great general (and grammarian) at the family home of the great poet:

> *valerium catullum a quo sibi versiculis de mamurra perpetua stigmata imposita non dissimulaverat satis facientem eadem die adhibuit cenae hospitioque patris eius sicut consuerat uti perseveravit* (Suetonius, *De Vita Caesarum – Divus Iulius* 73 xrl.us/bikitq)

> [Caesar] was satisfied to accept, on the very same day he was invited, the hospitality of, and a luncheon with, the family of Valerius Catullus, by whose little verses about Mamurra the stigma that attached to [Caesar] himself was ineradicable. The matter thus closed, [Caesar] continued enjoying their hospitality.

Cp. "Over Beers, No Apologies, but Plans to Have Lunch". *New York Times*, July 30, 2009 xrl.us/bmgfnu.

77. BBC, "On This Day: February 3" bbc.in/173M9.

78. Robert Kiener, "The Reader's Digest Interview: Paul Anka, Teen Idol", July 2011, p. 68 xrl.us/bmhpm9.

79. Wikipedia: "My Way"/Elvis Presley version: xrl.us/bmhsex.

80. Chadsey interview: "Macho, MotherMan, Men: Rethinking Masculinity", *Idiom*, January 14, 2011 xrl.us/bmhvgm.

81. The fictional Don Corleone of Mario Puzo's novel *The Godfather* views the adulterer as not a man of respect.

82. Cassius Dio Cocceianus, *Historiae Romanae* 62.13.1-2 (enumeration per Cary).

83. Cp. "As of November 10th, Sandusky is being investigated for allegedly 'pimping out' young children to wealthy donors of the Second Mile Foundation" in "Sandusky, Paterno, and the Devotion to Rape Apology", *Persephone Magazine*, November 11, 2011 xrl.us/bmx5ym.

84. Cp. this contemporary icon: xrl.us/bmxhyv.

85. The BBC seems particularly eager to engage in this practice: xrl.us/bmith8. Just in the time this note has been written, a BBC World News announcer has interviewed an economist from a European country that is experiencing fiscal difficulties. As the economist is explaining the rationale behind a surprise political maneuver by one of his country's leading political figures, the announcer interjects, "That sounds like an *Italian* level of deviousness!" (with a sliding upward inflection in his tone, as if political deviousness were something one would never expect of a non-Italian politician). The economist obligingly replies, his voice rising too, "It *is* Italian!" (though it is not).

A British MP, also, has recently performed this bit of semantic distancing: "Mild-mannered Murdoch shrugs off Mafia jibe", Reuters, November 10, 2011 xrl.us/bmif4g.

The New York Times has significantly lessened this practice on its pages in recent decades, though not eliminated it.

The antics of certain television personalities have not been helpful in this regard bit.ly/ukBEXM.

86. Holzberg (p. 30):

> [T]he Lesbia whose picture can be pieced together from the relevant poems of Catullus bears absolutely no resemblance to the likes of a Clodia Metelli, that is, to a female member of the senatorial class.

87. Wiseman (1987, pp. 135-36):

If [Catullus] didn't use obscenities in even the bitterest poems about her, he would hardly have introduced an obscene *double-entendre* into her name.

88. Cp. *Lesbian Vampire Killers* bit.ly/yCEEK.

89. Though I am emendation-averse, it seems to me that an *s* may have been lost *en route* to the extant manuscripts. In my reading of *Carmen* 48, *mellitos oculos tuos* (48:1) should be emended to *mellitum osculum tuum* or *mellita oscula tua*, depending upon whether read as singular, "your honeyed little mouth", or plural, "your honeyed kisses".

A mouth may taste sweet as honey; so may kisses. But, eyes are not flavored. Further, either form of *osculum* as the poem's second word would be book-ended neatly by the poem's last word, *osculationis*.

Support for the principle underlying this conjecture is to be found in this analysis by Wiseman (1974, pp. 60-61):

> [T]he ring construction is where the thought or phraseology at the end echoes that at the beginning. It could be done in various ways ..... The repetition may also be a key word or idea ..... This pattern appears most clearly in that most symmetrical of poems, 99, of which the first word is *surripui* and the last *surripiam*; poem 6 also has it, from *illepidae* in line 2 to *lepido* in the last line, as do poem 69, *noli admirari* (1) to *admirari desine* (10), and poem 114, *saltus* (1) to *saltum* (6).

90. Cp. The Crystals, "Then He Kissed Me" xrl.us/bhvwch. For interpretations, both innocent and not so, by several (male) scholars regarding what Catullus means by *passer, see* Gaisser, ed., pp. 305-340.

91. Cp. Rex Harrison, "Why Can't a Woman Be More Like a Man?" bit.ly/9EPEFD.

92. BB King, "In the Court of the King", *The Independent*, March 26, 2006 xrl.us/bmh33h:

> Many people have said to me, "do you have to pick cotton and suffer to play the blues?" And my answer is "No. But if you have, it helps." He roars with laughter.

Cp. BB King, "Every Day I Have the Blues" bit.ly/h5WSJb.

93. Thomson (2003, p. 294):

> *cogitationes*, 'thoughts' or 'observations', **often of a criti-cal sort**; in this sense, extremely common in Cicero, who uses it about 111 times. [Emphasis added.]

One can almost see the smirk on the face of New Poets refer-ring to Cicero by a Latin equivalent of "Mr Cogitations".

94. Cp. "Spotted Horses in Cave Art Weren't Just a Figment, DNA Shows", *New York Times*, November 7, 2011 xrl.us/b mij54.

95. To Green's credit, other Anglophone commentators, as far as I am aware, have not even raised this possibility.

96. *adulescentulum ... proceritas* <a tall young man>. (*Pro Caelio* 36 xrl.us/bimb5o)

97. Wiseman (1987, p. 65): "Quarrelsome, violent ... "

98. *See* Monaco generally xrl.us/bmcji2.

99. Thus David Mulroy (p. xl, n. 6): "It seems to me that in Poem 100 Catullus emphasizes his addressee's [*ie,* Caelius's] association with Verona precisely to distinguish him from his more famous namesake."[!] *See* also pp. 69-71 above.

This issue is a great concern in the physical sciences also; *see* "Scientific Retractions on the Rise", *On the Media*, Septem-ber 2, 2011 xrl.us/bmcjwe.

100. The premise, which is based upon *Pro Caelio* 5, is itself subject to doubt. Hejduk (p. 7, n. 11) notes: "The text in *Cael.* 5 is corrupt – that is, the place-name of Caelius' birth-place is not clear from the manuscripts."

101. "JAKARTA, Indonesia – President Obama was welcomed as a hometown [*sic*] boy made good – exceedingly good – when he arrived here Tuesday afternoon", in "Honoring the Presi-dent's Mother", *New York Times*, November 9, 2010 xrl.us/ bmcmvs.

Further, we do not know whether either or both of Caelius's parents have roots in Verona.

102. Until barely more than a century ago live performance, in one form or another, was the *only* form of entertainment for two or more people.

103. First Lady of the US, 1961-63; her official role as such cut short by her husband John F Kennedy's assassination. Thereafter, a glamorous and gifted editor and patroness. (The analogy is mine; it may not accurately reflect Skinner's view.)

104. If Catullus's (repeated) characterizations of Clodia's husband as impotent are true (from whom would Catullus have learned this, if not Clodia herself?), then Clodia's only documented long-term intimate relationship was with her brother Clodius. Whether such a close relationship between siblings (or other of Clodia's indulgences described by Cicero and Catullus) was "singular" relative to a woman of her position and place is itself open to question. *See* Suetonius, *Caligula* 24 xrl.us/bmbqf2.

105. Skinner (2003, p. 49) lists 11 instances.

106. *See Carmina* 3 xrl.us/bmfebk and 12 xrl.us/bmfebt.

107. My sense is that the Catullan corpus does not 'do' the same song-poem twice, and hence that *Carmen* 10's conclusion suffices as an instance of denouement at Catullus's expense.

Likewise, though for several centuries read as such by commentators, *Carmen* 35 is not a poetic representation of an actual social invitation, because, among several other reasons, *Carmen* 13 xrl.us/bmfeed serves that function.

108. *Pro Caelio* 25, 27, 49, 53, 56.

109. Consistent with the stereotypes about slaves held by an elite audience at a dinner gathering, Catullus caricatures the Door thus (Murgatroyd, p. 476-7):

> [I]t professes itself keen to please its master, at 9 ff. it protests its innocence and loyalty, at 11-14 it claims that it is badly done by, at 41 ff. it reveals itself as an eavesdropper and at 45 f. it is fearful, or pretends to be. Above all, as QUINN [*sic*] has commented (but without elaboration), it is the garrulous and gossip-loving type of slave.

In fact Catullus develops fully this latter aspect in a realistic portrayal incorporating characteristics that all readers will be able to recognize from their own experience of such types – the obvious relish for scandal of a sexual nature with intimate details [cp. classicists generally, as well as their students]; the tone of shocked disapproval (in 24, 25, 36 and 42); the readiness with which gossip is retailed (after a little prodding at 15-18, and after no prodding but merely vague encouragement in 29 f.); the signal that there is more to follow in *primum* [<*First ... *>] (19), gleefully picked up with the next instalment (*atqui non solum haec* [<And not only *that ... *>] etc., 31); the air of superiority as the speaker corrects a current misconception (19 ff.) and parades inside information (41 ff.); the sensational padding throughout 21-8; and at 45 ff. the conclusion with a juicy bit of scandal, built up by being cloaked with an aura of threat and mystery. And, to round out the personality still more, Catullus adds several not especially servile features, such as self-righteousness and sense of aggrieved dignity (9 ff.), the door's affection for its area of origin (34) and a rather showy penchant for 'poetic' and impressive turns of phrase (most notably in 21, 32-4 and 40 [...]). All in all, then, this is an elaborate, observant and quite subtle piece of characterization, and the door comes across as a real individual.

With similar psychological savvy, Woody Allen often strokes his own core audience's need to feel superior to those occupying a lower station in life. *See* especially *Mighty Aphrodite* (for which Mira Servino, in her movie debut, won a well-deserved Oscar) xrl.us/bkzhhh.

110. Thomson (2003, p. 465):

There is no reason at all why the Caecilius of this poem should not be identified with C's fellow-poet, who in Poem 35 is called, or perhaps recalled, to Verona by C from the embrace of his lady-love at Novum Comum ...

Note the parallel between the description of Caecilius II as *poetae tenero* <touching poet> (35:1) and Caecilius I as *dulci ... viro* <sweet husband> (67:1). As indicated earlier, each can be an indication of sincere affection, or a suggestion of a lack of manliness.

As well, there is no reason of which this reader is aware that the *virgo* <bride> of 67:19 should not be identified with the *sapphica puella / musa doctior* <Sapphic Mistress more knowing than a Muse> (35:16-17).

Likewise: the *Cornelius* of 1:3, 67:35, and 102:4. (*See* Appendix E.)

111. Some commentators read *quivis* <anyone> (67:16) as implying that the Interlocutor is accompanied by others, consistent with the Greek mode of *paraclausithyron*. At the least, it refers to a live audience and to future readers. Either or both readings have further support from a verse that follows: *nos volumus nobis dicere ne dubita* <Indubitably, *we* do! Tell us!> (67:18). Although often translated in the first person singular, *eg*, Green (2005, p. 167): "I want to, so tell me, don't be shy", by using the first person plural Catullus implies that his audience too, as well as future readers, want to hear the Door's version of events.

112. *tradita* in line 19 is often translated as "came", or the like (*see* pp. xii-xvi). But, in 67:9, *tradita* is clearly used in its more usual sense: the conveyance of property (there, the home originally occupied by Balbus). Since marriage at that time is likewise viewed as a type of conveyance of property (in this case, of a woman from her father to her husband), and since the legal conveyance of property is very much at issue here (hence the extreme measures to produce a male heir), I have retained this sense of *tradita* in both lines.

113. *beta* (67:21) means either "beet", or the second letter of the Greek alphabet (β). Translators have variously rendered *beta* here as "young beet" (Skinner 2003, p.47), "tender beet" (Leonard Smithers xrl.us/bmcuok), "beet root" (Green 2005, p. 167), *etc.* (*See* also xvi-xvii.)

I have chosen instead the Greek letter lambda (λ) as better evoking the image, for contemporary readers, of a *languidior tenera cui pendens sicula* <*little* dagger drooping limper than ...>.

114. That "celer" is embedded within *conscelerasse* <disgraced> may be mere coincidence; more likely it is an example of Catullus's characteristic playfulness.

Cp. *Pro Caelio* 60 xrl.us/bkjhqe:

> *ista mulier de veneni* celer*itate dicere audebit*

> *that* woman [spoken while pointing at Clodia, no doubt] will have the audacity to testify about *fast*-acting poison?!

Similarly, *caeco* (67:25) may allude to the Appius Claudius Caecus of Cicero's *prosopopoeia* in *Pro Caelio* 34.

115. *zonam solvere virgineam* <literally: to untie a girdle worn by a maiden (cp. the tamper-evident seal on a bottle of vitamins). I could not resist punning on *zonam*'s sense as "knot".

116. For a list of critics on both sides of the issue, *see* Skinner 2003, p. 203, n. 49.

117. *minxerit* literally means "micturated". But, the metaphoric meaning is translucent.

118. Oxford Latin Dictionary knows not the manuscript's *chinea* (67:32), and the evidence for *cycneae* as emendation is slight. My translation instead chooses "China", which at least is recognizable to modern readers.

119. Macleod (p. 188, with cites to Catullus, Kroll, and Ovid):

> [A]*dulter* and *adultera* can be used in a broad sense of illicit lovers, and anyway Postumius and Cornelius could have been married men.

120. ... *unless* Catullus is engaging in mockery of one of the persons he is alluding to in the song-poem (*ie*, Caecilius II, as shall be seen) – another reason why identifying the main characters in *Carmen* 67 should not be disregarded.

121. Green (2005, p. 65) translates *colonia* in *Carmen* 17 as "Verona" (correctly, in my view).

122. Cp. *veronam veniat novi relinquens / comi moenia lariumque litus* <Come [Caecilius] to Verona, relinquishing the walls of New Como and Lake Como's *shore*> (35:3-4).

Works Cited

Allen, Walter, Jr, 1937. "Claudius or Clodius?", *CJ* 33: 107-10.

Austin, Roland Gregory, 1950. *M. Tulli Ciceronis: Pro M. Caelio Oratio.* Oxford, UK: Clarendon Press.

Badian, Ernst, 1980. "The Case of the Door's Marriage (Catullus 67.6)", *HSCP* 84: 81-89.

Barceloux, Donald G, 2008. "Aconite Poisoning and Monkshood" in *Medical Toxicology of Natural Substances: Foods, Fungi, Medicinal Herbs, Plants, and Venomous Animals.* Wiley Online Library.

Bayle, Bernard, Lockman, *et al*, 1738. *A General Dictionary: Historical and Critical,* Vol. VII. London: James Bettenham.

Billanovich, Giuseppe, 1988. "Il Catullo della Cattedrale di Verona", *Scire litteras* = *Bayerische Akad. d. Wiss., Hist. Klasse, Abh. N.F.* 99, Munich: 35-57.

Blevins, Jacob, 2004. *Catullan Consciousness and the Early Modern Lyric in England: from Wyatt to Donne.* Hampshire: Ashgate Publishing Limited.

Carratello, Ugo, 1992. "Le donne veronesi di Catullo", *GIF* 44: 183-201.

Cary, Earnest (translator), 1925. *Dio's Roman History,* Vol. 8. London: William Heinemann.

Chan, Thomas YK, 2009. "Aconite Poisoning", *Clin Toxicol* 47: 279-85.

Chisholm, Hugh, ed., 1910. *Encyclpædia Britannica*, 11th Edition, Vol II. New York: The Encyclpædia Britannica Company.

Cilliers, Louis and Retief, Francois P, 2000. "Poisons, Poisoning, and the Drug Trade in Ancient Rome", *Akroterion* 45: 88-100.

Copley, Frank Olin, 1949. "The 'Riddle' of Catullus 67", *TAPA* 80: 245-53.

———, 1953. "Catullus 35", *AJP* 74: 149-60.

———, 1956. Exclusis Amator: *A Study in Latin Love Poetry.* Baltimore: American Philological Association.

————, 1957. Catullus – *The Complete Poetry*. Ann Arbor: The University of Michigan Press.

Crawford, Jane W, 1984. *M. Tullius Cicero: The Lost and Unpublished Orations (Hypomnemata)*. Göttingen: Vandenhoeck & Ruprecht.

Dane, Nathan, II, 1964. "Rufus Redolens", *CJ* 64: 130.

Dorey, Thomas Alan, 1958. "Cicero, Clodia, and the 'Pro Caelio'" in *Greece & Rome, Second Series*, Vol. 5, No. 2, pp. 175-80.

Evans-Grubbs, Judith, 1993. "'Marriage More Shameful Than Adultery': Slave-Mistress Relationships, 'Mixed Marriages', and Late Roman Law", *Phoenix* 47: 125-54.

Fordyce, Christian James, 1961. *Catullus: A Commentary*. Oxford, UK: Clarendon Press.

Fredricksmeyer, Ernst A, 1973. "Catullus 49, Cicero, and Caesar", *CP* 68: 268-78.

Gaisser, Judith H, ed., 2007. *Catullus* (Oxford Readings in Classical Studies). Oxford, UK: Clarendon Press.

Giangrande, Giuseppe, 1970. "Catullus 67", *QUCC* 9: 84-131.

Glare, Peter Geoffrey William, ed., 1968. *Oxford Latin Dictionary*. Oxford, UK: Clarendon Press.

Green, Peter, 1982. *Ovid: The Erotic Poems*. London: Penguin Classics.

————, 2005. *The Poems of Catullus: A Bilingual Edition*. Berkeley: University of California Press.

Gruen, Erich S, 1995. *The Last Generation of the Roman Republic*. Berkeley, New York, and London: University of California Press.

Hallett, Judith P and Skinner, Marilyn Berglund, eds., 1997. *Roman Sexualities*. Princeton: Princeton University Press.

Harrison, Stephen, ed., 2005. *A Companion to Latin Literature*. Malden, Massachusetts and Oxford, UK: Blackwell Publishing Ltd.

Hejduk, Julia T Dyson, 2008. *Clodia: A Sourcebook*. Norman: University of Oklahoma Press.

Holzberg, Niklas, 2000. "Lesbia, the Poet, and the Two Faces of Sappho: 'Womanufacture' in Catullus", *PCPS* 46: 28-44.

Kazazi, Mojtaba, 1996. *Burden of Proof and Related Issues: A Study on Evidence Before International Tribunals.* The Hague: Klewer Law International.

Keitel, Elizabeth and Crawford, Jane W, 2010. *Cicero: Pro Caelio.* Newburyport: R Rollins Company.

Kutzko, David, 2006. "Lesbia in Catullus 35", *CP* 101: 405-10.

Levine, Philip, 1985. "Catullus c.67: The Dark Side of Love and Marriage", *CA* 4: 62-71.

Lintott, Andrew William, 2008. *Cicero as Evidence: A Historian's Companion.* Oxford, UK: Clarendon Press.

Macleod, Colin W, 1983. "The Artistry of Catullus 67", in *Collected Essays.* Oxford, UK: Clarendon Press. 187-95.

Madsen, David W, 1981. "The Life and Career of Marcus Caelius Rufus", dissertation. University of Washington.

Merrill, Elmer Truesdell, 1893. *Catullus.* Cambridge: Harvard University Press.

Monaco, Matteo, 2008. *L'itinerario filologico di Ugo Carratello.* Rome: Aracne.

Mulroy, David, 2002. *The Complete Poetry of Catullus.* Madison: University of Wisconsin Press.

Munro, Hugh Andrew Johnstone, 1878. *Criticisms and Elucidations of Catullus.* Cambridge: Deighton, Bell and Co.

Murgatroyd, Paul, 1989. "Some Neglected Aspects of Catullus 67", *Hermes* 117: 471-78.

Noonan, John D, 1979. "*Mala Bestia* in Catullus 69.7-8", *CW* 73: 155-64.

Pasco-Pranger, Molly, 2010. "Speaking stone in Catullus 55", paper delivered at 106th Annual Meeting of the CAMWS.

Perlovsky, Leonid, 2011. "Language and Cognition Interaction Neural Mechanisms", *Comput Intell Neurosci* 2011: 454587 xrl.us/bmdpeq.

Perrin, Bernadotte, 1919. *Plutarch: Lives*. Cambridge: Harvard University Press.

Purser, Louis C, ed. (translator), 1903. *Epistulae, II: Ad Atticum, Pars Prior, Libri I-VIIII*. Oxford: Clarendon Press.

Quinn, Kenneth, ed., 1972a. *Approaches to Catullus*. Cambridge and New York: W Heffer & Sons.

———, 1972b. *Catullus: An Interpretation*. London: Batsford.

———, 2nd edition, 1973. *Catullus: The Poems*. London and Basingstoke: Macmillan and Co Ltd.

Rabinowitz, Jacob 1991. Catullus: Complete Poetic Works. Dallas: Spring Publications, Inc.

Reed, Edwin, 1902. *Francis Bacon: Our Shake-speare* [sic]. Boston: Charles E. Goodspeed.

Riggsby, Andrew M, 2002. "Clodius/Claudius", *Historia: Zeitschrift für Alte Geschichte*, 51(1): 117-23.

Richardson, Lawrence, Jr, 1967. "Catullus 67: Interpretation and Form", *AJP* 88: 423-433.

Rose, Herbert Jennings, 1921. "Catullus", *CJ* 16: 540-55.

Russell, Bertrand Arthur William, 1924. "Logical Atomism", in *The Philosophy of Logical Atomism*. DF Pears, ed., La Salle: Open Court, 1985, 157-181.

———, 1959. *My Philosophical Development*. New York: Simon and Schuster.

Shackleton Bailey, David Roy, 1971. *Cicero*. New York: Charles Scribner's Sons.

Skinner, Marilyn Berglund, 1981. *Catullus' Passer: The Arrangement of the Book of Polymetric Poems*. New York: Arno.

———, 1982. "The Contents of Caelius' *Pyxis*" CW 75(4): 243-5.

———, 1983. "Clodia Metelli", *TAPA* 113: 273-87.

———, 2002. "Transactions with Catullus", *CW* 95: 435-38.

———, 2003. *Catullus in Verona : A Reading of the Elegiac Libellus, Poems 65-116*. Columbus: The Ohio State University Press.

————, ed., 2007. *A Companion to Catullus*. Malden, Massachusetts and Oxford, UK: Blackwell Publishing Ltd.

————, 2010. *Clodia Metelli: The Tribune's Sister*. New York: Women in Antiquity, Oxford University Press.

Smithers, Leonard Charles, 1884. *The* Carmina *of Gaius Valerius Catullus*. London: Smithers.

Stern, Rex, 2010. "To Whom Am I Dedicating My New Little Talk? To Catullus and Nepos", abstract, 106th Annual Meeting of the CAMWS.

Tatum, W Jeffrey, 1999. *The Patrician Tribune: Publius Clodius Pulcher*. Chapel Hill: University of North Carolina Press.

Thomson, Douglas Ferguson Scott, 1967. "Catullus and Cicero: Poetry and the Criticism of Poetry", *CW* 60: 225-30.

————, ed., 2003. *Catullus*. Toronto, Buffalo, and London: University of Toronto Press.

Treggiari, Susan, 2007. *Terentia, Tullia and Publilia: The Women of Cicero's Family*. London and New York: Routledge.

Whigham, Peter, 1966. *Catullus: The Poems*. London: Penguin.

Wilder, Thornton Niven, 2003. *The Ides of March*. New York: HarperCollins/Perennial.

Wiseman, Timothy Peter, 1969. *Catullan Questions*. Leicester: Leicester University Press.

————, 1974. *Cinna the Poet and Other Roman Essays*. Leicester: Leicester University Press.

————, 1979. *Clio's Cosmetics: Three Studies in Greco-Roman Literature*. Leicester: Leicester University Press.

————, 1987. *Catullus and His World: A Reappraisal*. Cambridge: Cambridge University Press.

Zdrok, Victoria, 2003. "The Effect of Judicial Instructions on Jury Consideration of Defendant's Refusal to Testify", dissertation. Drexel University.

Index

Deus Pertundus (the Penetration God) *n. 64*

"Diana" (written and performed by Paul Anka, *qv*) 52

Dietrich, Marlene (*Witness for the Prosecution*) *n. 43*

diffamatio <defamatory song-poem> 79, 85, 91, 100, 122

Dindymian Domina (*see Magna Mater*)

Dio (of Alexandria) 21-3, 25, 28, 31

Dolabella, Publius Cornelius (Tullia's husband) *n. 65*

Domina <slave-mistress> 10, 68, 72-4; *n. 20*

Domitius Calvinus, Gnaeus (presided in trial of Caelius) *n. 47*

Dorey, Thomas Alan 24, 26

Dyson, Julia T (*see* Hejduk)

Egypt 21-4, 26, 28-9, 41, 65; *n. 46*

Ellis, Havelock 57, 61

Ellis, Robinson 80

Evans-Grubbs, Judith *n. 20*

fellatio (-atrix) 49, 51, 65-71, 81-2, 104

1st Triumvirate 11, 18, 20, 134; *n. 34-5, 39*

Fonteius, Publius (adoptive 'parent' of Clodius) 19; *n. 39*

Fordyce, Christian James v, 38

Formiae *n. 41*

Francis, Connie (Concetta Rosa Maria Franconero; "Who's Sorry Now") *n. 14*

Fredricksmeyer, Ernest A 6

Furius (likely literary rival of Catullus) 59-60, 67

Gaisser, Judith H *n. 90*

Gerron, Peggy Sue (*see* Holly, Buddy) 52

Giangrande, Giuseppe xiv, 43, 45, 90, 93-110; *n. 64*

Gigante, Marcello 130

Godwin, John 44

Goold, George P 44

Great Mother (*see Magna Mater*)

Green, Peter viii, 12, 43-7, 50, 70, 76, 80-1, 88, 99, 109, 115, 129-132, 135-8; *n. 5, 65, 95, 111, 113, 121*

Greene, Ellen *n. 19, 24*

Gruen, Erich 29-30, 145

Hallett, Judith P 60-64

Harrison, Rex (Reginald Carey Harrison; "Why Can't a Woman Be More Like a Man?") *n. 91*

Harrison, Stephen *n. 10*

Hejduk, Julia T Dyson viii, x-xii, 1, 11, 27, 38, 47, 50, 60, 76, 145; *n. 20, 100*

About the Author

Photo by Adriano Maffei; *Fabriano, Italia*

Gaetano Catelli was a Manhattanite from the moment of conception until the fall of 2010, when he permanently relocated to Oxford, Mississippi.

Elvis drew him to Mississippi; Faulkner drew him to Oxford.

There he continues to bicycle, make the acquaintance of charming ladies and stalwart gentlemen, sample from a wide variety of cultural offerings, study prime numbers from time to time, and work on his forthcoming biography of Clodia.